MARKETING TOURISM DESTINATIONS ONLINE

STRATEGIES FOR THE INFORMATION AGE

CONSEJO EMPRESARIAL **OMT**
WTO BUSINESS COUNCIL
CONSEIL PROFESIONNEL **OMT**

September 1999

Copyright © 1999 World Tourism Organization

Marketing Tourism Destinations Online

Strategies for the Information Age

ISBN: 92-844-0328-6

Published by the World Tourism Organization

The designations employed and the presentation of material in this publication do not imply the expression of any opinions whatsoever on the part of the Secretariat of the World Tourism Organization concerning the legal status of any country, territory, city or area or of its authorities or concerning the delimitation of its frontiers or boundaries.

FOREWORD

The Internet is having a greater impact on the marketing of travel and tourism than any technology since the invention of the television. It has already established itself as a crucial distribution channel via which tourism organizations can promote their destinations and products offered by their service providers. Yet it is still in its infancy, albeit growing-up fast.

The implications of the Internet and other growing interactive multimedia platforms for tourism promotion are far reaching. As we enter a new era, The Information Age, destination marketing organizations and other major providers of tourism services need to understand both the Internet and the other emerging interactive technologies, their increasing use by tourists and travellers and how to capitalise on these new channels. The benefits to be gained include cost-effective global distribution and new opportunities for closer and eventually self-financing partnerships between public entities and private operators.

Marketing Tourism Destinations Online – Strategies for the Infomation Age has been written with this in mind. The report's objective is simple: to be a single, authoritative source of information that will provide guidance to destination marketing and other tourism organizations in how the online world is developing and how all the public and private parties involved might participate and so reap the benefits.

The WTO Business Council hopes that this book will contribute to the future development of marketing tourism in Cyberspace and that it will assist those tourism organizations and private operators wishing to embrace the new opportunities of online promotion and distribution presented as the world enters the new era of the Information Age.

The WTO Business Council would also like to express its appreciation and thanks to our member MasterCard International, whose sponsorship made the financing of this study possible.

Martin Brackenbury
Chairman
WTO Business Council

José Luis Zoreda
CEO
WTO Business Council

CONTENTS

MARKETING TOURISM DESTINATIONS ONLINE   i

Strategies for the Information Age   i

FOREWORD   iii

ACKNOWLEDGEMENTS   viii

CHAPTER 1:   *INTRODUCTION*   *1*

CHAPTER 2:   *ONLINE TRAVEL DISTRIBUTION – A HISTORICAL REVIEW*   *7*

Introduction   7

How the Airlines Created Global Travel Distribution   7
    The Diversification of the GDSs   9
    Global Financial Framework   11
    Case Study: IATA BSP   11

Accommodation   13
    Case Study: Pegasus Systems and TravelWeb   16

Chartered Air Travel   18

Cutting Out the Middle Man   20
    Case Study: easyJet   21

CHAPTER 3:   *THE DAWN OF THE INFORMATION AGE*   *23*

Introduction   23

The Origins of the Internet   24
    How the Internet Works Today   26

Consumer Take-Up of the Internet   27

Other Current Online Technologies   34
    Interactive Digital Television   35
      What is Digital Television?   35
      What is the Potential for Digital Television?   36
      The Potential for the Travel Industry   37
      Why the Potential of IDTV will be Fulfilled   39
    Case Study: ntl   39
    Case Study: Travel Channel   41
    Net Appliances   43
      Network Computers   43
      Game Consoles   43
      Set-Top boxes   43
      Mobile Telephone and Computer Units   43
      Screen Telephones   43
    E-Ticketing   44
    Case Study: United Airlines   45

CHAPTER 4: TRAVEL AND TOURISM – ONLINE AND ON-SALE   47

Introduction   47

Travel and Tourism Consumers Online   48
Browsing Travel Web Sites   51
Online Travel Industry – 1998 Figures   52
European Online Travel Industry to Boom   52
Online Hotel Bookings   52

Private Sector Travel on the Web   53
Case Study: American Express   56
Case Study: STA Travel   58
Case Study: Sportscar Tours   59
Case Study: Kuoni Travel   61
Case Study: Forte Hotels   65

Destination Marketing Organizations, IT and the Internet   66
Towards the Internet   67
The Increasing Use of IT by DMOs since the mid-1980s   67
The Internet– New Opportunities for DMOs   67
Towards pro-active use of the Internet by DMOs   68
DMOs and Internet Commerce   68
Tourism Value Chains, Old and New   69
Destination Management Systems – An Overview   69
An Integrated Approach to the Use of IT   69
Destination Management Systems and the Internet   70
Other applications of an integrated DMS   70
The Strategic Challenge   71

New Entrants in Travel and Tourism Intermediation   73
The Internet Portals   75
Case Study: Microsoft Expedia   76

CHAPTER 5: DMO TECHNOLOGY CASE STUDIES   81

Introduction   81
Case Studies and Evaluated   81
Evaluated Only   81
Reviewed Only   82
Overview of 25 DMO Web Sites Evaluated   82
Introduction to Key Features   82
Special Features and Demonstrations of Good Practice   84

Web Site Case Studies   88
Zurich   88
Background   89
Western Australia   90
Background   91
Enjoy Cornwall   92
Background   93
Singapore   94
Background   95
Spain   96
Background   97
VisitBritain   98
Background   98

Destination Management Systems   100
The Austrian TIScover System   100

Overview of Key Features 100
Rationale 100
History 101
Current status 101
Data Management 102
Distribution 102
Financial Aspects 102
Specific Strategies and Issues 102
Conclusions 103
The Finnish Tourist Board Systems: MIS, PROMIS and RELIS 103
Overview of Key Features 103
Rationale 103
History 104
Current Status 104
Financial Aspects 105
Related Systems 105
Conclusions 106
The Irish Gulliver System 106
Overview of Key Features 106
Rationale 106
History 107
Current status 107
Financial Aspects 107
Specific Strategies/Issues 108
Conclusions 108
Namibia Wildlife Resorts Central Reservation System 109
Rationale 109
History 110
Current Status 110
Financial 111
Specific Strategies and Issues 111
Conclusions 111
Canadian Travel Exchange (CTX) 111
Overview of Key Features 112
Rationale 112
History 113
Current Status 113
Financial Aspects 114
Specific Strategies and Issues 114
Conclusions 114
South Pacific Islands Travel Channel 114
Overview of Key Features 114
Rationale 115
History 115
Current Status 115
Financial 116
Strategies/issues 116
Conclusions 116

CHAPTER 6:   STEPPING INTO THE INFORMATION AGE   117

Introduction   117

Developing a Presence on the Web   117
The Role of the Internet within the Overall Marketing Strategy 117
Specifying the Web Site Functionality 119
Preparation of a Structure and Design 120

Contracting an Agency 121
Origination of Product Information in Digital Form 122
Production of Editorial and Graphical Material 123
Testing/Evaluation of Pilot Site 124
Implementation, Monitoring and Evaluation 125
Promoting the Use of your Web Site 126
    Promote the URL 126
    Obtain Links from other Sites 126
    Search Engines 126
Critical Success Factors 127

Developing a Destination Management System **128**
DMS Critical Success Factors 129

Purchasing Travel in the Information Age **130**
Intelligent Agents 132
Buyer Driven Commerce 134
The Role of Smart Cards 135

CHAPTER 7: CONCLUSIONS **137**

Introduction **137**

The Winners and Losers **137**
New Strategic Threats 138
    Competitive Rivalry 138
    Buyers 139
    Suppliers 140
    Potential Entrants 140
    Substitutes 140
The New Electronic Marketplace 140
The Losers 141
The Winners 142

How DMOs May Evolve **143**
Opportunities for Public/Private Partnership 144

Possible Roles for the World Tourism Organization **145**

The Final Word **146**

TECHNICAL GLOSSARY **147**

APPENDIX 1: ANALYSIS OF 25 'BEST PRACTICE' WEB SITES **151**

URLs of Web Sites Evaluated **151**

Aggregate Analysis of the Sites Overall **152**
Aggregate Analysis of the Functions and Services Offered By 25 DMO Web Sites
Evaluated 153

Individual DMO Web Site Analysis **156**

APPENDIX 2: INDICATIVE COSTS TO PARTICIPATE ONLINE **167**

DMO Internet Web Sites **167**

Destination Management Systems **167**
Scenario 168

ACKNOWLEDGEMENTS

The World Tourism Organization Business Council would like to thank Paul Richer of Genesys – The Travel Technology Consultancy and Roger Carter of Tourism Enterprise and Management along with their colleagues for the excellent preparation of this report.

We have received much assistance from the organizations featured within the case studies in this report and are grateful to them for allowing themselves to be included and for making time to be interviewed.

We would also like to thank those research organizations who have provided statistical information for inclusion in the report.

CHAPTER 1: INTRODUCTION

This document contains many technological terms. Explanations of these can be found in the Technical Glossary at the end of the report.

As recently made evident during the last World Tourism Organization conference on "Measurement of the Economic Impact of Tourism", held June 1999, travel and tourism is the world's largest industry. It continues to show consistent year on year growth with worldwide arrivals growing 4.3% per annum between 1989 and 1998. In 1998, 625 million tourists spent $445 billion (excluding international transport). The chart below illustrates figures for the last five years:

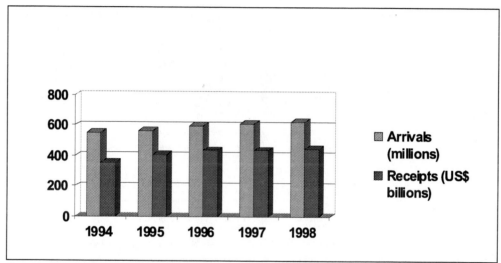

Source: World Tourism Organization

According to research undertaken by the World Tourism Organization, the growth trend will continue. Its forecast, Tourism: 2020 Vision, shows tourist arrivals increase by over 200% between the years 2000 and 2020. The split of inbound arrivals by regions is predicted to be as follows:

Forecast of Inbound Tourism by Region			
(international tourist arrivals in millions)			
	2000	**2010**	**2020**
Europe	386	526	717
East Asia/Pacific	105	231	438
Americas	131	195	284
Africa	26	46	75
Middle East	19	37	69
South Asia	6	11	19
Totals	**673**	**1046**	**1602**

Source: World Tourism Organization

In 1997 tourism receipts accounted for just over 8% of total world exports of goods and almost 34% of total world exports of services. Whilst the travel account balance in developed countries as a whole has been in decline since 1980 (a surplus of just $0.8 billion in 1997), the balance in developing economies has been consistently in surplus growing from $33.7 billion in 1989 to $62.2 billion in 1997.

The following chart illustrates the trend:

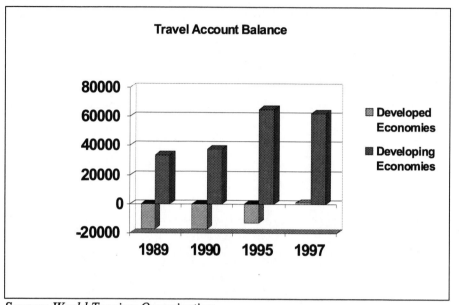

Source: World Tourism Organization

It is clear from the figures that there is a consistent flow of tourists from the developed to the undeveloped economies. Where are they originating from? The top 4 tourism spenders are the United States, Germany, Japan and the United Kingdom. In 1997, these four countries alone accounted for 41% of tourism expenditure.

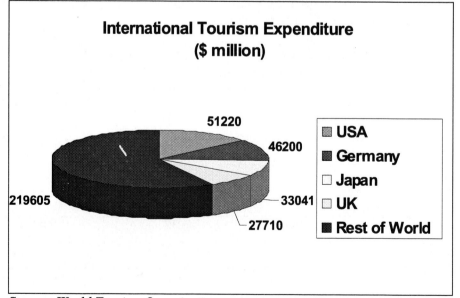

Source: World Tourism Organization

This is particularly significant because these countries are spearheading the world's entry into the new era of The Information Age. Having moved from the Stone Age, through the Iron Age and into the Age of Industrialisation, the world is now entering an era where information is the commodity that is shaping peoples' lives. With the advent of the fax machine, mobile telephony and now the Internet, the world's population is becoming accustomed to instantaneous global communication; and communication is not just about people contacting each other. Communication is also about the delivery of information, including tourism information, and it is those countries that spend the most on tourism that also have the highest number of Internet users. The next chart shows the number of Internet users from the same top four countries that spend the most on tourism.

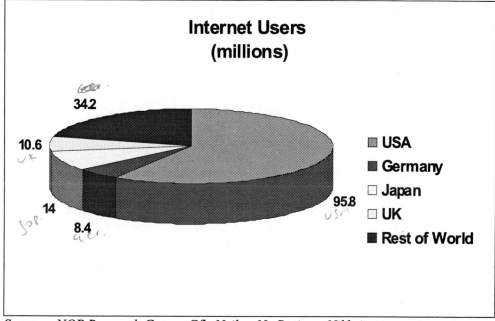

Sources: NOP Research Group, Gfk, NeilsenNetRatings, Nikkei

These four countries USA, Germany, Japan and United Kingdom, account for 79% of the world's present Internet population (128.8 million users).

As we move into the Information Age, consumers' expectations are being radically altered. The Internet, more than any other technology, is teaching people that they can go online and quickly find out about any subject that is currently holding their interest. Not only can they obtain a substantial depth of information, they can do this instantaneously. Consumers in the Information Age are no longer satisfied with requesting information and then awaiting its arrival. They are expecting instant information gratification. They are learning fast that the Internet can satisfy this.

Why is this important to the travel and tourism industry? It is because the industry's products do not exist when they are purchased. When travel is bought it is typically no more than information on a computer reservation system. What the traveller is buying is the right to the product, an airline flight or hotel room, at some time in the future. Travel is information at the point of sale. Unlike most consumer goods such as televisions, cameras and cars, travel cannot be sampled before the decision is made to buy it.

This is also true of tourism's product.   It cannot be sampled before the traveller arrives.   Thus, the decision to "purchase" the destination, that is to visit it, is based solely on information made available to the tourist.   This may be recommendations from friends, it may be brochure material supplied by National Tourism Offices or perhaps advertisements.   Increasingly, however, it is information made available on the Internet, particularly on the World Wide Web.   Tourists are tapping into the wealth of destination material on the World Wide Web and using this is a primary source of destination information.   The new truth for destination marketing organizations is that **if you are not online then you are not on-sale** within your key markets.

If your destination is not on the Web then it may well be ignored by the millions of people who now have access to the Internet and who expect that every destination will have a comprehensive presence on the Web.   The Web is the new destination marketing battleground and if you are not in there fighting then you cannot expect to win the battle for tourist dollars.

Participating on the Web is absolutely essential but it does not have to be a daunting task to do so.   DMOs can embrace the Information Age and, whilst it is possible to invest millions of dollars in doing so, this need not be so.   A good presence on the Web can be developed at surprisingly low cost.

The World Wide Web is the ideal channel for promotion of destinations.   It is a global medium.   It costs no more to distribute information to a continent on the other side of the world than it does to a neighbouring region.   It is a multi-media experience.   (Multi-media is a term used to describe information being delivered in a variety of formats.   Those that are most used by the Web are text and images - graphics and photographs.   However, the Web can also deliver sound and video and these media are becoming increasingly used to provide a rich audio-visual experience.)

If you are competing, then one of your weapons is quality of information. Tourists will primarily base their decisions about which destinations to visit on the information available to them.   If one DMO can better represent its destination on the Internet than another then it may win the tourist who is uncertain about where to travel.   To compete, the successful DMO must provide a better information experience than its competitors.

One of the key challenges for DMOs is to build a database of multi-media destination information that can be utilised for online promotion.   A presence on the Internet cannot be developed if there is no base information to place on a Web site.   Information collation and management is a primary task of the DMO.   This must be comprehensive, held in electronic formats, and needs to be constantly verified and updated.

Once a suitable depth of information is available electronically, this can be utilised to build a Web site.   It can also be made available to tourist information centres within your region or country.   Thus, the DMO begins to build an integrated information systems strategy whereby a single source of information is used both internally to the DMO's organization and externally on the Web and in partnership with third parties.

Who are these third parties? They are the private sector companies such as specialist tour operators who are selling travel to your destinations, as well as the service providers who are providing products such as accommodation. Search for any destination on the Web and hundreds of links to Web sites will be found. Many of these will be promoting your destination and they may be doing this well or badly. The challenge for DMOs is to assist private sector organizations promote their destinations in the best possible way. This may be by providing access to an online library of information which is free of any copyright restrictions if used to promote the destination but perhaps there is further scope for DMOs to assist the private sector.

If a DMO's Web site has become the information gateway to its destination, should it facilitate contact between visitors to its site and private sector organizations that sell travel products and services to and within the destination? If it is facilitating such contact, should the DMO be paid commission by private sector companies for business that it has sourced? Should DMOs own their own commercial inbound tour operations? These are some of the questions that arise when one considers how the marketplace will develop in the Information Age. There may be no single strategy that is right for all DMOs. Whereas Gulliver in Ireland has been completely privatised (see the case study in Chapter 5), other DMOs may wish to limit their partnerships with the private sector in order to maintain neutrality between all service providers within their destinations.

As more and more consumers worldwide adopt online distribution channels as their preferred way of buying travel products, so the industry will change. A new breed of global travel vendor is entering the market. The new electronic distribution channels are a boon for these new entrants. They need not invest in the physical infrastructure of the traditional high street retail agent and, in theory, can operate from a single office, a garage or spare bedroom.

All they need to succeed is access to customers. The new players may be Internet search directories like Yahoo!, Excite or Lycos, or software companies like Microsoft and Netscape. If they have pre-existing online customer relationships, it is viable for them to invest in a new online travel vending business serving those customers. The new players may also have new ways of selling. Auction sites where the customer sets the price are becoming increasing popular with those seeking value for money when buying travel products (see the section on Buyer Driven Commerce in Chapter 6).

There are four types of new travel company evolving. The first is a huge, global player; acquiring smaller competitors in order to achieve great economies of scale, companies such as Carlson in the US or Airtours in Europe. In a perfect market, there can only be one giant low cost winner, able to undercut all the others. In the real world, several of these giants can co-exist, being kept apart by imperfect market barriers of geography and consumers' lack of perfect knowledge.

The second type is one that which has recognised that the customer relationship is king. Whether it is a department store such as Marks & Spencer, a retailer like Walmart or an entertainment corporation such as Disney, it will own and capitalise upon a trusted relationship with the customer. This intermediary will diversify from its core product into low physical infrastructure products such as finance and travel.

The third type is the portal. This intermediary owns the customer's connection to the world. It is a cable television company such as Cable & Wireless or NTL, or an Internet search engine. Whenever its customers go online, it is via their portal and this yields the opportunity to sell electronically delivered products, such as travel, to the customer.

There is a fourth type of intermediary that has been in existence for many years and will continue to thrive. This is the niche player. The small company that has specialist knowledge or sells a specialist product. For example, travel agents and tour operators that specialise in a particular destination. Consumers will always do business with organizations that understand their specialist needs and it should be the task of DMOs to support those specialists who are selling their destination.

These niche players are no longer constrained by the cost of breaking through geographic barriers. The niche player can now tackle global markets. For just a few hundred dollars of Internet Service Provider charges and with some careful planning and design, world markets can be captured by organizations which, a few years ago, could not have contemplated looking beyond their own borders. Global distribution is available to the smallest players (see the Sportscar Tours case study in Chapter 4).

The challenge for national, regional and local tourist boards, as much as for other destination marketing organizations, is to move with the times and enter the Information Age. This challenge can be met. Reading this report may be your first step or you may already be online and on-sale. Regardless, you will benefit from a greater understanding of the new market environment and discover how other travel and tourism organizations are tackling the challenge. You will learn about the World Tourism Organization Business Council's Vision for the New Millennium, its vision for Destination Marketing in the Information Age.

CHAPTER 2: ONLINE TRAVEL DISTRIBUTION – A HISTORICAL REVIEW

INTRODUCTION

This chapter reviews the birth of online travel distribution. The historical background provides a setting for what is happening today and what is to take place in the world of travel and tourism online. It explains how the Global Distribution Systems (GDSs) came into existence, why they have dominated the online distribution of travel products and why they may continue to do so.

Whilst the GDSs originally provided a booking capability for just scheduled air seats, they have now expanded to encompass a range of bookable travel products including cruise, car rental and accommodation. The accommodation (or hotel) sector has been particularly keen to obtain distribution via the GDSs and has introduced its own systems to help link to the GDSs. The way in which this has been achieved is also reviewed in this chapter.

Charter air travel has never been bookable on the GDSs and yet brings so many tourists to new destinations. Because of its importance to tourism, the distribution of charter air travel is also examined.

Of course, it is the goal of many travel principals to sell direct to the customer, cutting out the middle man and saving the payment of commission. Before the Internet, this was not easily achieved. Now, however, many organizations are placing the Internet at the heart of their distribution strategy, having realised that there are enormous savings to be made. Selling direct is reviewed in this chapter, including a case study about an airline, easyJet, that was launched purely as a direct sell operation.

HOW THE AIRLINES CREATED GLOBAL TRAVEL DISTRIBUTION

When, over thirty years ago, Sabre created the first airline computer reservation system (CRS), charter airlines were run on a far smaller budget than their schedule airline siblings and did not possess such a developed structure for distribution either. Today we refer to the CRSs as the global distribution system (GDSs). However, in spite of the growth in charter traffic, electronic travel distribution still retains its bias towards the schedule air industry, belying it origins from this period. The evolution of GDSs resulted in a major shift in the way that we buy and sell travel around the world. The GDSs developed from the schedule air industry's need to provide an easy method by which travel agents could sell their products. An agent with a GDS terminal can instantly check availability and make a booking on behalf of a customer.

Specifically, four GDSs facilitate the global travel distribution market, as the following diagram illustrates:

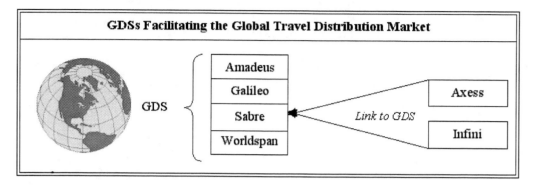

GDSs Facilitating the Global Travel Distribution Market

The Japanese Axess and Infini systems are linked through Sabre either directly or through locally hosted systems.

Amadeus is the largest GDS organization, with its operations including many of its partners' and owners' internal airline reservation functions. It was founded over ten years ago out of the break-up of the European GDS consortium by four airlines: Air France, Iberia, Lufthansa & SAS. The first three still remain as controlling partners, however SAS has left this grouping (yet retains local marketing of the Amadeus brand) and within the period Continental Airlines has also joined the partnership. Amadeus' distribution is handled within local markets by national marketing companies (NMCs) who mostly trade under the Amadeus branding.

Galileo operates a similar distribution system to Amadeus in the sense that local management of services and marketing is delegated to national distribution companies (NDCs). However, Galileo has now undertaken a policy of acquiring charge of its NDCs. Galileo was founded in its current form around the same time as Amadeus, as a partnership between British Airways, KLM, Air Canada, US Air (now US Airways) and United Airlines, whose hosted system, Apollo, they chose to incorporate. Smaller additional European partners included Aer Lingus, Alitalia, Olympic Airways and Swissair.

Sabre has been owned since its foundation by the parent organization of American Airlines, AMR Corporation. Conceived in the early 1960s, Sabre is seen as the forerunner of the modern GDS. It operates a Corporate Travel System and call centres. It is one of the largest airline hosting companies in the world and until recently was the only GDS to operate an Internet travel agency - Travelocity. Sabre has expanded its operations through an undertaking with ABACUS to service the Asia-Pacific markets. It has also been involved in the outsourcing of US Airways' technology services.

Worldspan was formed from the merger of Delta Airlines (DATASII) and PARS (whose parent companies are TWA & Northwest Airlines). The previous partner of ABACUS (before Sabre), it is considered the smallest of the four GDSs. It operates mostly within the US, but has a subsidiary in London which controls all non-American affairs.

The circumstances in which the GDSs have operated have changed in recent years. At the inception of the systems, they favoured their parent airlines by listing their flights in front of all others on availability displays when particular routes were queried by travel agents. This bias was tolerated because of the huge investment undertaken by these organizations to implement their systems. They needed to recoup their capital.

However legal moves forced the airlines to divest themselves of controlling interests in their GDSs and so remove the bias on flight availability displays. This has led to stock market flotations by some of the GDSs and to others considering this as a possibility. In October 1996, Sabre was floated on the New York Stock Exchange (NYSE) with an initial public offering (IPO) of 20%. Approximately 18% of this was sold to private investors. Galileo was floated in the US by its partner-owners in 1997, who have undertaken to buy back the stock held by the airlines. Amadeus has also expressed a desire for an IPO to list on the Madrid Stock Exchange.

The situation that now exists is that the GDSs are larger and more public entities than they ever were. Their global reach has expanded from their initial markets and has even provided growth for their individual owners. To ensure a deeper and more efficient market penetration, the GDSs are creating stronger organizations through mergers and allegiance building and by seeking further distribution agreements. This has led to more efficient operations and a reduction in costs due to economies of scale, because the capital investment in technology can be spread over these larger organizations.

In building a more functional and efficient technology, the GDSs have adapted the most worthwhile core functionality of their systems. One method has been to incorporate these into a more modern interface or a database system. Another has been to increase functionality by creating electronic links between systems to facilitate greater amounts of information available to a greater number of users across the merged organizations. Overall the schedule airline GDS of today is a much more efficient animal than its predecessor, but it is still clear where its roots lie. The next section looks at how the GDSs have diversified away from purely distributing scheduled air although their technology is still best suited to this activity.

The Diversification of the GDSs

As with all businesses, the GDSs cannot afford to rest on their laurels, but have been seeking to extend and diversify their business offerings in more recent times. They have already set the standard within their particular field, naturally appealing to travel agents trained to use their systems. Therefore, the way to diversify the range of products on offer is to extend the services already sold. This has not been an easy route to take because the GDS is optimally designed to facilitate air travel transactions.

The infrastructure already in place is one that is not easily accommodating of diversification within its product base. Overall, only 10% of revenue brought in by the GDSs comes from non-air products. Hotel accommodation and car rental are examples of extensions to the GDS which have had some limited success. Of hotel products, only around 10% are available on the GDSs. Car rental does much better, with around 40% booked via this channel, but there is still a majority that remains unbookable. To make up for this, some of the local distribution systems (such as START in Germany) offer products such as tours, or rail and ferry services. These are bookable away from the traditional GDS structure, in separate windows, as the core passenger name record (PNR) system employed by the GDSs cannot facilitate them. However, these market specific products cannot be considered an all-out success, often proving to be cumbersome to administer for their operators. Examples of this type of system are US based products such as TourSource, LeisureShopper (tours) and Cruise Director (cruises).

One of the great difficulties of GDS technology is that it has not been easy to use. It has been usual to see dumb terminals or non-user friendly text based systems, requiring a high level knowledge by the user of the appropriate technological syntax. This is costly both in terms of time and operator training. The GDSs employ many people, specifically as trainers, for the purpose of ensuring travel agents are fluent on their use. A move to more user friendly Windows style systems, with drop down menus and appropriate options within fields, has removed the degree of technical knowledge needed to operate the GDSs and indeed means that the operators do not actually need to have a knowledge of the GDS syntax whatsoever. Such technological diversification has opened up the opportunity for Internet based solutions to begin appearing. Already Galileo allows business users to specify their own bookings via the Internet, which are then sent to their preferred travel agent for administration and ticketing. These types of systems are key examples of how the GDSs are helping to support travel agents, whilst continuing to improve efficiency.

In whichever direction the GDSs move forward, one undeniable truth is that they need to be operating within the online travel market. Inevitably, with any such business extension, there is debate on the best way to move forward. Galileo and Amadeus, in spite of Galileo being a partner in Internet Travel Network (one of the top US online travel agencies), have committed publicly to not competing directly with their travel agent customers. Worldspan is approaching the situation in a different manner, and is trying to become the back-end technology for online agencies through its involvement in MSN Expedia and Biztravel.com. Sabre openly competes in the online direct sales market with its own travel agency, Travelocity. Sabre has also created a corporate travel agency system called BTS as a complementary product to Travelocity. In this venture they are partnered by Carlson Wagons Lits and BTI America, two corporate travel agencies in the US.

The direction of the diversification and extension of the business of the GDSs, and their technological progression, are clear. Moves towards a less technologically savvy user base, coupled with moves into the online travel markets, are indicative of an industry seeking to make itself more efficient and appealing. A greater width of product base within this more user-friendly Windows/Web based environment provides a more complete solution within the GDS environment. The GDS environment itself is ideally suited to a global technological infrastructure, such as the Internet, and therefore it is unsurprising to find moves by all the GDSs towards becoming major players in the sale of travel products on the Web.

Global Financial Framework

Since the days of Thomas Cook Travel Group and his temperance tours, we have been using tickets as instruments to facilitate our means of travel. It is a common practice which is still in use today.

The bulk of airline tickets are still issued on paper in spite of the existence now of electronic tickets. Travel agents broker these tickets which are representative of the right of transportation and effectively exist as a form of currency until they are exchanged for travel. The airline ticket is a commodity of value until redeemed and can be seen as a negotiable instrument of commercial value, rather than simply as a ticket to ride.

The common unit of exchange and a method for controlling the ticket system commercially is provided by IATA (International Air Transport Association) and the American ATA who have set the standard for ticket content and layout. Today we use internationally accepted tickets as representation of our right to travel. Because travel has progressed to such a degree, it is no longer appropriate for single tickets to be representative of a single type of transport and, ideally, tickets should be multi-modal, allowing the traveller to hold a single ticket that might, for example, encompass a journey on rail, air and bus. However it is still the case that barriers to fluid inter-modal transfers remain. Even with the existence of electronic funds transfer (EFT) many travel distribution networks still employ antiquated economic transaction systems that are not suited to handling travel transactions for all forms of transport. Nevertheless, in the world of air transport, the financial transaction systems devised and administered by IATA and ATA have allowed travellers to book multi-airline flight itineraries which require just one ticket and, for the traveller or his agent, one financial transaction.

Case Study: IATA BSP

(International Air Transport Association Bank Settlement Plan)

Before the International Air Transport Association (IATA) introduced its global IATA agency programme in the 1950's, each individual airline needed to provide its own ticket stock to agents and to financially settle on an individual basis. The IATA programme was designed to produce an IATA ticket stock and provide a central forum to which accredited travel agents and airlines could administer financial transactions in bulk utilising a centralised clearing system – the IATA BSP (Bank Settlement Plan) which settles international financial transaction between airlines and travel agents. Today this system is being used in 61 countries around the world. A powerful body, the IATA BSP facilitates the co-ordination of policy formulation between the agencies and the airlines. It is the system which allows the IATA programme to function.

The IATA BSP is a non-profit making organization, which outsources ticket distribution, data processing and the bulk purchase of ticket stock to contractors whose charges are passed on to the airlines and agents who use the service. Hence the IATA BSP can be seen as a central forum for the framework within which the air travel industry operates. Its full remit of global settlement services includes:

- Sales reporting and remittance processing

- Commission disbursement

- Banking

- Funds transfer and electronic payments

- Document procurement and distribution

- Credit card billing and settlement

- Sales outlet identification

- Certification and accreditation

- Management and marketing statistics

- Global communications services

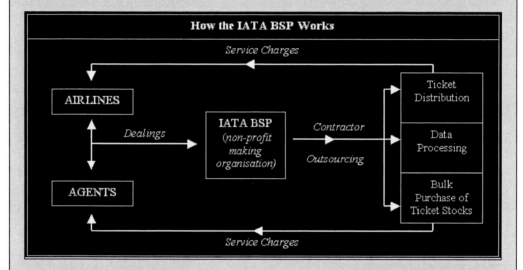

It provides digital billing information for accounts and marketing to use. This also allows data processing centres within each company to calculate how much each agency needs to submit to the central clearing bank and to inform those banks of the necessary clearing settlements. This system is a success, handling worldwide net sales in 1995 of $77 billion, with dealings between 286 airlines and over 43,000 agencies.

The natural progression for the IATA BSP system would be to introduce ticket stock applicable to products other than simply air travel. IATA wishes to create a fully integrated multi-modal ticketing system. Already they have convinced the GDSs to use the existing ATB printers within agencies, which provide extra revenue to help keep down the airline's costs. This ideology, coupled with the GDSs desire to expand their product base, makes such a system a likelihood rather than a mere vision. BSP UK, for example, has expanded its non-airline products already to include railways and ferries. Ticket stock now includes Eurostar and British Rail (ATOC) and has the potential to spread to all rail operations.

The BSPs predominantly operate within local markets, servicing for the most part the national services. However, this regionalisation stands in the way of the IATA programme to create a centralised BSP processing system to improve efficiency and reduce costs which is more in line with the strategy of the GDSs to provide global reservation facilities. The body designed to facilitate this change is the IATA Distribution Service (IDS) which is trying to create regionalised standards.

It is e-ticketing (electronic ticketing) that is ultimately seen as the means to reduce the overall cost of transactions. IATA has created standards in electronic data interchange (EDI) in accordance with the United Nations guidelines on this issue. This provides a standard for the production of e-tickets for airlines and agents who wish to use these.

However advances in this area are limited not simply by technological constraint, but by cultural ones as well. The move to an entirely electronic system, rather than the traditional methods, would be a culture shock to those passengers who prefer the comfort of holding a physical ticket. In spite of this, e-ticketing remains an attractive option, removing much of the manual processing and hence enabling cost savings to be achieved.

The strategy for the future of IATA BSP is to increase its product base and facilitate the processing of all forms of travel transaction. By creating an automated direct sales system that is electronically processed, IATA can end the concept of manually processing tickets. In spite of the obvious advantages to this, problems may come when trying to encourage agents to move to automated systems as, under European anti-immunity laws, IATA cannot restrict access to its programme based on non-automation. Smaller outlets may not feel it a financial benefit to automate and may insist on manually processing tickets. This would continue to cause IATA to employ staff to manually enter this data.

Whilst changes to the system might be slow, there is a past precedent for eventual substitution. ATB2 – the newer generation of paper ticket stock – was in planning for many years before its introduction. Lufthansa has already introduced smart card technology on two of its German routes, albeit it seems a long way off before this is widely implemented. (A smart card is a credit card sized card that contains a micro-chip to store information – far more than can be stored on the usual magnetic stripe found on most credit cards.) IATA has already considered the possibility of cyber-accredited online agents (existing without premises or staff). However the consensus is that such a degree of automation is still years off. Ultimately though, electronic transactions and automated systems that improve efficiency and remove the antiquated manual processing system must be seen as the end goal for IATA.

ACCOMMODATION

Whereas the GDSs have been successful in distributing air travel, this has not translated into similar success in non-air travel markets. It is still the case, even in the United States, that the majority of hotel and car rental bookings are non-GDS. For the most part, the hotel industry relies on direct contact with customers for distribution, or on a local company to administer for them. However, hotel bookings bear certain key similarities to air-travel products that make it interesting to examine why a GDS type service has not worked so well in this sector. Firstly these types of product are all finite in terms of time. They are perishable. Once their time has past, the opportunity to sell the products has gone. Secondly both air travel and hotel rooms are usually only incidental in the framework of business travel to the main reason for travelling.

The distribution methods for these seemingly similar products remain largely distinct. The majority of hotel bookings are sold either locally or through direct, repeat business. The standard hotel marketing model is, therefore, to target these areas more than trying to create new business. The key distribution methods are:

- Through hotel directories

- Via promotion in printed media

- Pre-selling (via tour operators) – as risk is effectively transferred, this is done at a reduced cost

- 'Walk-in' business

- Direct marketing

What is clear though is that a system such as the air travel GDS has not been implemented for the hotel industry and that it does not have such a natural application as it does for the air travel industry. By examining why this has not happened it is possible to learn whether there might be a future application for a GDS type distribution system designed specifically for the accommodation sector.

Hotels are very individualistic and the products which they sell are not standard. Selling a hotel product on an electronic system would involve a much more detailed description than a standardised product such as an airline ticket. Traditionally for hotels this has been achieved through print media. Attempting to show the description of a hotel product on a very limited GDS display, with categories such as 'luxury' rather than full descriptions, is very limiting. GDSs, in technological terms, have not been able to display pictures or offer detailed descriptions outside of category designator.

Hotel transactions are far more complex than airline products. Consideration not only has to be given to the alternative accommodation at a particular venue, but also in the surrounding area. The amount of data needed for such as system could not be held by the type of technology currently employed in GDSs. In respect of technological problems there are two major considerations:

1. Connectivity – hotels have found that sophisticated systems and effective connectivity have proven financially prohibitive. To achieve a system as worthwhile in its usage as the air industry GDSs would not prove to be financially worthwhile to the hotels. This situation is especially the case for independent hotels, which would make up the majority of product inventory on such a system.

2. Cultural problems – Hotels have found that even if connected via a central reservations office (CRO) to a GDS, travel agents prefer to book or confirm over the phone. Even worse, they might book on a GDS but confirm by telephone, doubling the cost of the reservation.

One of the major issues raised here is that the majority of hotels operating are independents. Of all the properties that make up the total accommodation stock, over 90% are considered smaller properties (defined as less than 50 rooms). These types of establishment rely mostly on local sales and traditional forms of distribution. Their targeting and characteristics are local and therefore not realistically suited to a GDS.

In order to consider how this situation might change in the future, so making the implementation of some GDS type structure more appropriate, it is important to note firstly why major shifts are occurring in the hotel environment, and secondly what these shifts are.

There is already evidence of structural changes within the hotel industry. For instance, there has been a rapid expansion of hotel groups. These are gaining in popularity because of the improved opportunities afforded to such groups. They can benefit through economies of scale with their distribution. There is an argument to suggest that with increases in sophisticated technology, there is greater opportunity for direct marketing channels (such as the Internet). These groups can now employ the skills and capabilities to utilise numerous distribution channels. After all, efficient methods of distribution are crucial to the travel industry's strategic business processes. Growth through new distribution channels opening up (such as the Internet) and technological improvements to the GDSs mean that for these groups, the distribution structure traditionally employed by the hotel industry is certainly changing.

In the resort hotel sector, a large proportion of business comes from the mass market tour operators. Some hotels will be completely contracted during peak season and not require any further distribution. Hence for this sector, there may be less reliance on travel technology. Greater numbers of people utilising direct online methods of distribution will not change the situation dramatically. In spite of many of these resort hotels being represented on the Internet themselves or through associated organizations with Web sites, the expectation is that most bookings will still come through the traditional channels. In this way, tour operators can package other elements to the hotel product to create an entire holiday solution.

Those who wish to directly market themselves online face a huge dilemma. They cannot afford to alienate the tour operators by offering cheaper deals, yet cannot gain direct sales without offering competitive rates.

In summary, even though there are key similarities to air travel products, hotel products possess their own characteristics, usually spatial, that mean a GDS is not the most appropriate distribution solution. Hotel products provide a greater number of options to the traveller than the standard air travel product. However, technological advances and the emergence of larger hotel groups provide a scope for development in this area. It is unlikely that hotel products will become standardised and describable in terms of simple categories but technological solutions, such as being able to display pictures or being able to transport brochure documentation over the Internet, will make electronic distribution a more realistic option.

Case Study: Pegasus Systems and TravelWeb

Pegasus Systems Inc. provides electronic commerce and transaction processing services to the hotel industry worldwide. Pegasus originated during the 1980s at which time a range of technological solutions to traditional hotel booking processes were beginning to emerge. Up until the late 1980s, travel agents had made hotel bookings over the phone or via telex, a time consuming and costly process. Availability once confirmed could later be withdrawn, sometimes taking up to two weeks to complete. The airlines had already made pioneering moves during the 1960s with the introduction of computer reservation systems (CRSs) now known as global distribution systems (GDSs). As a natural extension of automated air distribution, the GDSs began to link-in the larger hotel CRSs (central reservation systems) during the late 1980s. However, agents while experiencing an improvement in the booking process could still not gain direct access to the hotel's CRS. Consequently their room requests would lie static on the GDS for a period of time thus increasing the likelihood of an invalid booking.

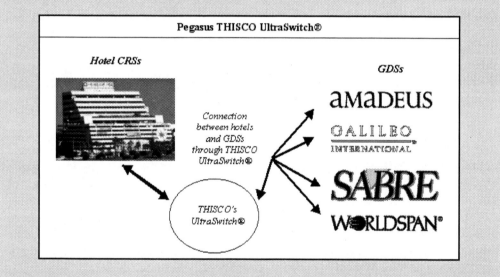

To overcome these inadequacies and look at new ways to reduce distribution costs, 15 major hotel companies, with the necessary resources to support the agent, co-operated in 1988 to form The Hotel Industry Switch Company (THISCO) from which UltraSwitch, a standard interface, was borne in 1989. UltraSwitch today connects 28,000 hotels to each GDS including; Galileo's 'Inside Availability', Worldspan's 'Hotel Select', SABRE's 'Direct Connect Availability' and Amadeus's 'Complete Access Plus' providing low cost access to more than 300,000 travel agencies worldwide. However, the International Hotel & Restaurant Association (IHRA) estimated in 1997 that despite 21% of all hotel bookings worldwide originating from the travel agent, only half of these are booked using a GDS. This percentage is expected to improve, as has already been the case in the US, with agents seeking to improve earnings in the aftermath of airline commission capping.

Some of the larger hotel companies derive up to 80% of their agency distribution via the GDSs. The last three years has seen Pegasus Electronic Distribution GDS transactions increase at a compounded annual rate of 29 percent. The 'next generation' of technologically savvy agents will help to further increase GDS bookings, aided by improvements in training and support. However servicing these bookings involves the hotel chains in paying agency, GDS, CRS and credit card fees.

1992 saw the establishment of the Hotel Clearing Corporation (HCC). Known today as Pegasus Commission Processing this service automated the process of agency commission payments. Today over 23,500 properties and 82,000 travel agencies in 206 countries participate. 1994 subsequently saw the launch of TravelWeb, one of the first online Internet travel catalogues aimed at the consumer, corporate buyer and travel agent direct. In 1995, TravelWeb.com became the first travel site to accept online hotel bookings. By 1999, TravelWeb.com featured nearly 26,000 hotels in 170 countries accessible in real time via the THISCO switch now known as Pegasus' Electronic Distribution System. TravelWeb.com also includes airline booking capabilities and an area called 'Click it! Weekends' where hotels can distribute perishable last minute stock at guaranteed low rates. Capitalising on their position as the leading electronic hotel transaction player, Pegasus also launched Pegasus IQ and Driving Revenue into a new business unit called 'Pegasus Business Intelligence', supplying a range of benchmarking and custom compiled analyses to the industry.

TravelWeb.com seeks to reduce distribution costs by serving the needs of those consumers that would otherwise book direct through traditional channels. TravelWeb.com's online distribution database and booking engine forms the backbone of Pegasus Electronic Online Distribution (formerly known as Netbooker), a private label system used by third party sites such as Preview Travel, MSN Expedia in the US and more recently Recruit Co. Ltd in Japan. This offering has also given 31 hotel companies the opportunity to provide own branded sites eg. Hyatt.com and Sheraton.com. Pegasus' online distribution database enables hoteliers to achieve their Internet distribution objectives providing support for the flexible representation of logos, images, brochure information and related content which can be updated at any time, allowing rapid reaction to market changes.

In 1998, Pegasus processed 21.5 million electronic GDS reservations or approximately $3.5 billion worth of hotel room sales. From $2.4 million sales per week sold over the first seven months of 1996 Pegasus' Internet distribution channels had achieved an average of $3.2 million sales per week (air and hotel) by the second quarter of 1998. 80% of those Internet bookings originated in the US. During the first quarter of 1999, Pegasus' Internet hotel reservations were triple that of the same period in 1998. GDS reservations processed in the first quarter 1999 increased 48.0% over the same quarter of 1998, although this was in part attributable to new participants such as Bass Hotels and Resorts.

Whilst Pegasus clearly leads the way in Internet hotel distribution with approximately 85% share of all Internet hotel sales, total transaction revenue is expected to increase significantly against a predicted doubling of the total market to $1.1 billion in 1999 (PhoCusWright, Inc). Pegasus is constantly looking at ways to meet the needs of the market by developing new ways to automate the distribution process for different segments. This has included plans to offer services to the convention and corporate travel segments with research underway into voice recognition technology. Aimed initially at the in-house groups market, voice recognition technology could further simplify and speed-up hotel transactions.

According to PhoCusWright, in 1998 online distribution intermediaries generated just over $230 million hotel bookings. TravelWeb.com alone accounted for approximately $50 million of those bookings. These intermediaries accounted for 44% of all online hotel bookings during 1998. That share is expected to increase to 51.3% by 2001 leaving 49% sold through hotel branded sites. Of the estimated 360,000 hotels worldwide, approximately 50,000 or 14% benefit from electronic distribution. Until now, the other 310,000 have not been able to effectively compete within the electronic marketplace and/or did not have many options to choose from without significant cost. The Internet is effectively enabling Pegasus to launch a new product, code named 'WebBook', to allow these typically small to medium sized hotels anywhere in the world to compete electronically with the big chains for the first time. Full details of the product are yet to be released but all participants will need is a Pentium PC, Internet connection and an ISP. Potentially destination marketing organizations (DMOs), working with organizations such as Pegasus, can help to extend local suppliers' distribution access, in a way that had previously been seen as impossible and/or inefficient, by integrating seamless connection to each participating supplier on their existing DMS (Destination Management System).

Until 1999 DMOs could pursue one of two strategies. Firstly, to build their own booking engine with separate inventory or secondly to utilise a traditional intermediary. Pegasus looks to be one of the first intermediaries to offer a comprehensive real time 'Web' solution which can also fit within the framework of a DMO's existing DMS strategy. In addition, individual DMO members can choose whether they wish to participate.

Among the first DMOs expected to pilot systems of this nature is the Denver Metro Convention & Visitors Bureau (www.denver.org). Approximately 70% of their hotel members are already featured in the Pegasus online distribution network. The remaining 30% will be able to sign up for the new service and not only take advantage of real time reservation capabilities on the Denver site but also be onwardly distributed to the 50 plus distribution channels within the Pegasus network. There are approximately 432 CVBs in the United States of which 350 had established Web sites by early 1999.

In summary, hotel distribution is progressing towards a series of interactive online partnerships lessening the overall dominance of any one portal. Pegasus continues to meet the needs of these entities, exploiting three in-house core competencies including electronic distribution, commission processing and business intelligence. The outlook is clearly changing in terms of whether GDSs are a true reflection of electronic travel distribution. According to HEDNA, (Hotel Electronic Distribution Network Association) while net GDS hotel reservations continue to rise, that growth has fallen year on year since 1995. The majority of bookings currently undertaken through traditional media by the consumer direct, such as the telephone, is where Pegasus expects to see the most significant amount of change in the next millennium.

CHARTERED AIR TRAVEL

In terms of electronic distribution, chartered air travel is significantly different from scheduled air travel. Chartered air travel primarily originates in Europe. This is primarily because many countries, in a bid to support their national airlines, have in the past imposed severe economic and regulatory restrictions on airline traffic between countries. In spite of this, the sheer demand for travel has been far in excess of the capacity that these national airlines have been able to supply and other airlines have been able to operate in the arena of mass market leisure travel. As a result, many airlines have grown up around business from the budget conscious travel market and are subsidiaries of the major tour operator groups. These include Britannia Airways (a subsidiary of Thomson Holidays), Corsair Group (France) & Hapag Lloyd Group (Germany). The market for these airlines today is a healthy one, with millions of travellers being transported at prices much lower than the equivalent scheduled fare.

Chartered airlines mainly operate by selling seats in blocks direct to tour operators or through agents who purchase a commitment to fill a number of seats and so share risk at a reduced cost. This system meant that there was little need for very sophisticated management or inventory controls. Seats were rarely ever sold on an individual basis, but as blocks of seats or as whole aircraft to operators or other groups. From the point of view of electronic distribution, the growth in GDSs did not really take chartered air travel into consideration. Although today the GDSs do not ignore this area, they still have the issue of how best to display what stock remains for a particular flight on a GDS. The problem is that multiple airlines might be listed several times on a GDS display for a single aircraft. Currently the rules restrict this to two airlines in a single neutral display. Yet for the chartered air market, this issue is not just about multiple representations, but also about in which order they should be listed. For instance, should Air 2000, who issue most of the seats on their flights, be listed first on the GDS display or should this privilege go to the other risk takers who have bought blocks of seats?

This situation is made even more complex when other factors are added to the equation. Currently the sale of seat-only (as opposed to within packages) is growing all over Europe and accounts for almost 20% of chartered flight sales. This trend is expected to increase as there has been a growth towards more independent travelling – that is to say travelling outside of package deals. This removes what was once a clear distinction between scheduled and chartered traffic and indeed today some flights carry both scheduled and chartered passenger loads. Obviously the standard and traditional categories upon which the GDSs relied have become more complicated and harder to facilitate. An example of where this has happened is perhaps best found by examining the market for North Atlantic discount traffic from Germany, which is now over 80% scheduled. The trends towards seat-only packages means that scheduled traffic can entirely fill up chartered aircraft as the fares are now so similar and customer servicing has been significantly improved – previously something which clearly differentiated the two types of air travel. What has happened is that the transatlantic charter service has been destroyed by scheduled services. Only some niche markets, mainly in the Caribbean, such as to Cuba, Dominican Republic or Cancun, have been able to retain any significant chartered air travel service.

The GDSs aided this change, primarily because they are more suited to scheduled air travel transactions. The trend towards more independent travel occurred at a time when the GDS technology was changing to allow fully integrated systems, rather than a multitude of separate systems. Today the actual application of these systems – pioneered by the Belgian organization, Wirtz – has facilitated the consumer's purchase of travel products through direct interrogation and innovative aggregation. An example is the French travel company, DegrifTour, which sells exclusively through either Minitel – the French system of interactive terminals installed in consumer households – or the Internet. The application of such systems may dictate the direction of this market in the future. However, this is one area where technology may be seen to be directly helping to shape the market.

CUTTING OUT THE MIDDLE MAN

When Southwest airlines first emerged in the US during the early 1970s, few at that time could have realised the ensuing impact. Southwest introduced low cost air travel to the market, increasing competition and subsequently drove down the cost of flying. Southwest brought air travel within the reach of a wider market not only in terms of price but also with improved direct access over the telephone and such early innovations as the installation of self-ticketing machines in 1979.

However the extent to which travel principals such as airlines can sell direct remains debatable. While Southwest became a model for low cost carriers around the world, the cost of servicing direct bookings also started to come under closer scrutiny. As rivals in the market place fought back, travel agents continued to play an important role in air travel distribution. During the late 1990s, Southwest's agency commissions per ASM (Available Seat Mile) remained relatively unchanged against rising credit card processing, communications and systems costs.

Direct selling has nonetheless become widely apparent within other sectors. For example in the United Kingdom, package holiday industry tour operators have experienced increasing direct sell demands. One company in particular, Direct Holidays, based its marketing proposition on bypassing the agent and became an important acquisition for Airtours during 1998. Yet even within this sector Price Waterhouse Coopers 1999 ABTA (Association of British Travel Agents) benchmarking survey suggests limits to direct sell.

Clearly much depends on the complexity of the product and the availability of expertise either in or out of house to meet the needs of the consumer. Intermediaries can help travel principals lower their operating costs by bulk distribution, streamlined technologies and value adding activities. For example, agents are increasingly introducing service fees for low cost or non commissionable products. Airlines such as easyJet, Go and Ryanair, offer no commission to agents. Yet a number of online bookings come from agents who charge their clients a service fee. Typically, low cost air travel involves ticketless point-to-point fares. Putting the necessary systems in place online to make those products bookable is relatively easy when compared with the diverse range of complex products on the market such as tailor made long haul.

A critical success factor in the next millennium will be the extent to which information technologies can form the basis for more complex on line interactive travel services for both direct and business to business transactions. This will inevitably bring travel principals back to the implications of Saffo's dis-re-intermediation, ie. the extent to which new and innovative traditional intermediaries can capitalise on lowering the cost of distribution while at the same time providing additional value adding services.

Case Study: easyJet

Founded in October 1995 by a Greek citizen, Mr Stelios Haji-Ioannou, easyJet has helped to mobilise a cultural shift across Europe towards direct sell, low cost and reliable air travel. Against this background the company has successfully grown its operation from two United Kingdom routes servicing London Luton Airport to Edinburgh and Glasgow, to 22 routes across Europe, in a little under four years. The airline caters for both the leisure and cost conscious business markets. Strategically, easyJet is committed to having one of the world's youngest fleets which will include eighteen aircraft by the end of 1999, fifteen further 737-700 series from July 2000 followed by the option to utilise another fifteen.

The carrier has a diverse mixture of customers who are primarily budget orientated. One of easyJet's unexpected market impacts has been its ability to attract business travellers. easyJet has sought to encourage all customers to book early for cheaper deals while also promoting Internet special fares. Each new easyJet aircraft has the airline's familiar telephone number on one side and the Web address on the other. During peak periods customers are pushed towards the Web-site whilst queuing on the telephone.

In September 1998, easyJet ran a promotion in The Times newspaper which generated one million pounds of business in the first day, 40% of which went through the Internet site. In late 1998, easyJet set a target of reaching 30% Internet bookings by the end of 1999. This figure had already been achieved by June 1999 raising expectations of reaching 60% for the millennium. In one week, 31 May to 6 June 1999, easyJet sold over 17,000 seats online. Every Internet booking directly saves the company an 80p tele-sales fee and the cost of transferring incoming calls from outside the UK. A few bookings are also coming in through travel agents who subsequently charge the customer a service fee. The company is also moving towards a more aggressive marketing approach, with links from Internet service provider sites and from easyEverything (Internet cafés) and easyRent (car rental).

Data-mining techniques (analysing sales in search of buying patterns and trends), employed to improve load factors, have been a key element in achieving rapid growth. easyJet's philosophy towards yield management has always been to match supply with demand. As a general rule, this means encouraging customers to book in advance. Customers booking immediately before departure are likely to pay a higher fare although still at a competitive rate.

The airline has succeeded in retaining an energetic, entrepreneurial mindset with over 50 managers, 250 direct-sell telephone agents, 150 pilots and 200 cabin crew. Wherever possible, work is outsourced with the focus of the company on keeping costs to a minimum. With this in mind, easyJet was early to realise the power of open, flexible systems. OpenSkies, a US based reservation system supplier, provides the core reservation system with direct links to easyJet's Web site. The reservation system has done well up until now, proving flexible and expandable. Hewlett Packard acquired OpenSkies in early 1999.

Already operating in a paperless office environment easyJet has been quick to innovate where costs can be saved. The IT department recently constructed its own voice over IP (Internet Protocol) link with Athens after being unable to obtain the same service through the Greek telecommunications company. Further challenges have involved integrating TEA's systems (an easyJet franchise) with Luton where the company has succeeded in further centralising IT operations, providing personalised systems access via a Citrix metaframe server running windows NT.

This has not only enabled the company to reduce costs associated with remote stations but, more importantly, simplified the integration of other systems. For instance one development under investigation is the 'Paperless cockpit' running over secure IP providing 'pilot weathering' and a host of operational advantages. The system could also allow easyJet to integrate tailored destination information in the passenger cabin.

Opportunities for DMOs to work with companies like easyJet and promote tailored low cost products in new ways are likely to arise early on in the next millennium. For instance, providing customers with the ability to send and receive data at 'no cost' could not only help strengthen easyJet's appeal to business travellers but also create further value adding and revenue generating possibilities onboard and in terminal.

easyJet is certainly one of the many travel companies that are making effective use of the technology of the Information Age.

CHAPTER 3: THE DAWN OF THE INFORMATION AGE

INTRODUCTION

We are at the start of a new era. The end of the 1990s will be remembered as the dawn of the Information Age. With the advent of mobile telephones in the 1980s, the Internet at the beginning of the 1990s and now interactive digital television (IDTV), we have reached the start of an era where consumers take for granted instant global communication and instant access to information.

However, whereas the technology appears impressive, it is still intrusive with PCs being the devices primarily used to access the Internet. Before too long, a PC will no longer take-up space on a desk and be complicated to use. It will no longer require a keyboard, responding to voice only. Over the next ten years, expect computing and the online transmission of information to become normal facets of everyday living that are taken as much for granted as the television and the fax machine.

Computing and communications will become transparent to the everyday user. Access to the Internet will be via the Net Appliance, a device that will be as simple to use as a television. Some form of screen device may sit on your breakfast table, ready with the morning newspaper already downloaded. You may use your telephone to send and receive e-mail. Your television will undoubtedly provide access to the Internet and the World Wide Web.

In this new Information Age, access to data on travel and tourism will be taken for granted. Prospective tourists will research destinations online. They will not wish to travel until they have the comfort of detailed information on where they are going. Those destinations that win will be those that can satisfy this thirst for information, that can convince the tourist online that their destination and the products that can be experienced there are worth the time and expense of visiting.

This chapter looks at the dawn of the Information Age, examining the origins of the Internet, how it came into being and how it developed to the stage which it is has now reached.

An important aspect of the Internet is the vast number of people who are now connected. Nearly all these people are also tourists. They can now use the Internet to reach out across the globe to take an online look at the places they wish to visit. Therefore, this chapter also reviews consumer take-up of the Internet. Who is using it? Are they the type of people who travel frequently? Are they the tourists who may wish to visit your country, your region?

Of course, whilst the Internet is very important, it is not the only online technology in use. Interactive digital television (IDTV) has been launched in several markets. In those markets where it is being introduced, industry analysts are expecting it to bring more people online than those using PCs to access the Internet. These people will be surfing information, at ease from the comfort of their living rooms. IDTV, therefore, is also reviewed in this chapter, as is the Net Appliance, the newest and possibly to be the most popular way of connecting to the Internet.

This chapter also provides an overview of E-Ticketing. The E-Ticket (Electronic Ticket) is the last piece in the jigsaw of selling travel online. Purchasing a flight online with an airline that has introduced E-Ticketing means that there is no paper based document that must be delivered to or collected by the traveller. When E-Tickets roll out to international travellers and become widely adopted, this will make travel a pure electronic product.

THE ORIGINS OF THE INTERNET

From the 1930s, telex networks allowed people to send text down the wire and since the 1970s, data as well as text can be sent over the telephone network. We have, therefore, been in a connected world for many years. However, it is only in recent years that the Internet has brought global connectivity to mass consumer markets worldwide. In fact, the Internet is not a new technological phenomenon but has been around for 30 years or more.

It originated from the Advanced Research Projects Agency (ARPA) - a scientific body set up by the Pentagon in 1957 - and its research into networking. This led to the military ARPAnet, the precursor to what we know today as the Internet, which was designed to create a message system that didn't rely on a single route. If one node (computer) was destroyed, then messages could still get through. This was called CCC or C3 (Command, Control and Communication). Exchanges could re-route the information to its destination via alternate nodes. The computers along this route could 'talk' to each other, even if they were not compatible, because they relied on protocols (the languages of computing) that were platform independent.

What was just described is essentially a switch network. In terms of telephony, it is called circuit switching. In the late 1970s and early 1980s, for the transfer of data, this came to be called packet switching, the premise being that there does not need to be a complete connection from one end to another. Packet switching allows a piece of data to try and find a way through to its final arrival point, stage by stage, not straight from source to destination. This is a store and forward system. A message is sent, stored and then sent again when the next stage is free and so forth, until it finally arrives. Packet switching breaks one large piece of data into smaller packets. The router attaches a header to a packet, so the information can be sent as many packets through different routes. This increases the overall speed of transmission and the capacity of the networks. At the last staging point, they wait at the exchange to go to the final destination. The packets are assembled at the final exchange in the process of being delivered. This whole system took many years to develop, primarily in the United States.

At some point towards the end of the 1960s the Internet as we know it today entered academic use. In December 1969, the fourth node was added to an academic network in the United States as an education tool on the ARPAnet structure. This event is the precursor to the modern day Internet. From this point onwards, the Internet has grown at a phenomenal rate and the velocity of this growth has not yet reached its apex. For example, ten years after this event, 188 nodes were in operation Ten years after that, it had grown to approximately 159,000. In July 1997 that figure was 19,540,000. Originally the Internet was supposed to be a tool for heightened production and wide-scale programming efforts. What it became was a communications tool for academics over long distances, for discussion and information transfer. Any and all types of information could be sent from one node to another, and it didn't matter where people were located – in the next room or on the other side of the world.

E-mail and the Internet first appeared publicly in 1972 at the Internet Computer Communications Conference. By 1973/74, the communications protocol that allows all computers to communicate was created, in what is essentially its current form – TCP/IP (Transfer Control Protocol / Internet Protocol).

ARPAnet was not the only interconnected network (Internet) to emerge and in 1989 NSFNet (National Science Foundation Network) superseded it. Originally it was a US government project but very soon it was turned over to commercial business and today remains what is referred to as the 'backbone' of the Internet.

The 1990s have brought commercialisation to the Internet. In 1993 the White House went on the Net and since then millions have joined them. Systems for domain name registration – Internet addresses - were commercialised in 1995 and the predominant form of transferring information moved to local interconnected providers – Internet service providers. The later part of the 1990s has brought with it a greater public awareness of the Internet. Indeed Microsoft's flagship operating system, Windows 98, was released with a greater emphasis on the Internet than ever before. It is now usual to see Web addresses on adverts. Commercial successes such as Amazon.com and E-Bay are listed on the international stock exchanges. The chart below illustrates the growth in the World Wide Web, where commercial companies market and sell their wares to consumers.

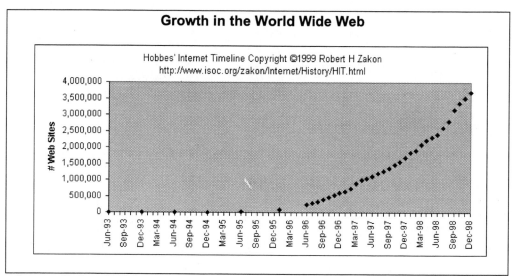

Source: Robert H Zakron

E-commerce has begun to come of age and Internet access is now freely available across much of the world. The ethos of the Internet is still the same as it ever was and its roots clearly lie in its past. However the possibilities for the future of an interconnected, networked society are being expanded and explored every day. From not so humble beginnings, we can at least predict with relative certainty that the future of the Internet will be of greater expansion and functionality.

How the Internet Works Today

When considering the Internet, it is important to understand that essentially it is simply a set of protocols that allow any computer to 'talk' to any other computer. The Internet is not platform dependent at all. It does not rely on being operated on one particular make and model of hardware or under one type of operating system. This means that these protocols can be adhered to from any system - from the standard home Windows based computer to the most expensive super computers – and over any type of network – from the telephone network to the cable based systems being used by cable television. The protocol is known as TCP/IP. When a computer adheres to this protocol it can be connected to the Internet. For the vast majority of home users, the telephone networks around the world are the only truly global network to which they have access and so they connect to the Internet in this way. These connections give a relatively low speed of access because only a certain amount of data is allowed to flow through the telephone lines. These users 'talk' to other computers via a modem (modulator - demodulator) which interprets the digital information of a computer and converts it to sound. This sound is then interpreted by the receiving computer's modem and converted back into digital information. Usually home users connect to an Internet Service Provider (ISP) such as CompuServe or AOL which may be a local or international organization. ISPs provide high speed networks to connect to sections of the Internet not held on their servers.

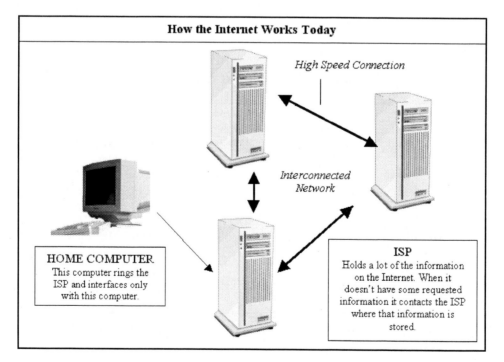

How the Internet Works Today

High Speed Connection

Interconnected Network

HOME COMPUTER
This computer rings the ISP and interfaces only with this computer.

ISP
Holds a lot of the information on the Internet. When it doesn't have some requested information it contacts the ISP where that information is stored.

Those who have been using computers for many years will remember a time when to use a computer you needed to understand complex syntax entered into a punch card or text only interface that was bare and harsh to use. However modern operating systems are graphically driven allowing the user to 'drag and drop' using a mouse rather than having the need to enter unnaturally worded commands. The same is also true for the Internet. Today we 'surf the net' with easy to use Web browser software such as Microsoft's Internet Explorer or Netscape's Navigator. Before the Internet became as sophisticated as it is today, the retrieval of information had to come from commands written in a complex syntax.

In 1989 the World Wide Web (WWW or Web) was created at the 'Conseil Europeen pour la Recherche Nucleaire' (CERN), today known as the 'European Laboratory for Particle Physics'. Most people today consider that the Internet and the Web are the same thing. This is not true. The Web is a system by which people can easily manoeuvre themselves around the Internet. Although it is still possible to use the Internet without the Web, just as it is still possible to use a PC through DOS instead Windows, most people operate within the confines of a browser.

The Web conforms to what are now commonly accepted standards. The key to the Web is hypertext. Hypertext is perhaps best described as the language in which the Web is written. Its most common flavour is HTML (Hypertext Mark-up Language). although more sophisticated versions, such as XML (eXtensible Mark-up Language), exist and are being advanced all the time. Within Hypertext it is possible to display Web pages as long as they conform to the standards of the browser in which they are being displayed. As browsers are advanced (we are currently up to version 5 of Microsoft's Internet Explorer), they allow more complicated pages to be displayed. However the beauty of the Web is that it has to conform to universal standards and so most browsers will be able to display the information presented in a useful form, even if the browser is an older version. Whilst it would be naive to consider that the Web is faultless, without it the Internet would not be accessible to most people, nor would it be as useful as it is today.

There are multiple uses for the Internet and although these are expanding almost every month, it is worth further examination into the major uses for the Internet today.

CONSUMER TAKE-UP OF THE INTERNET

Why do people want to be on the Internet? For any new technology to succeed it must possess some real worth, otherwise consumers will not adopt it. Although the Internet is not a new technology, it being accessible to the home user is a relatively new phenomenon. This has not just expanded its use, but has also expanded its scope. Before the 1990s (actually before 1993) the Internet was used as a tool for communications, primarily through e-mail, discussion groups, long-distance communications and long-distance file transfers. There was a sense of freedom about the Internet, the participants able to act in an unregulated fashion. Effectively the Internet was an example of a successful anarchic society. However as the 18th century philosopher, Rousseau pointed out, once past a certain size, any society can no longer exist in non-competitive harmony. Towards the end of 1992 under 20,000 domain names had been registered. Today this figure is well over 1,500,000. A larger consumer take-up of the Internet has added new dimensions to this original model. As can be seen from the following chart, an increasing proportion of US households that are computerised are going online.

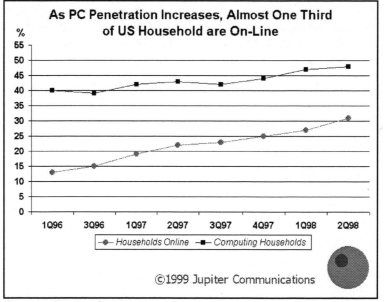

Source: Jupiter Communications

The later part of the 1990s has brought commercial interests to the Internet. It is unusual to see larger organizations without a Web site today. Companies, at the very least, want to maintain a Web presence, whilst others seek to do business on the Internet through e-commerce. The reasons for enthusiasm in this technology are obvious. Whereas real-world distribution or marketing involves huge investment, the online world promises much smaller overheads and potential global penetration.

With more and more people joining the online community, the commercial possibilities for the Internet are becoming very apparent. The amount of money being spent through the Internet is growing exponentially, with predictions from ActivMedia for Internet generated revenue totalling over $1,200 billion by 2002. These figures are calculated in two ways. By considering the growth in the number of Internet users and also by trying to predict at what level consumers will accept e-commerce into their lives in the next few years. The next chart illustrates one research organization's prediction of the growth of Internet generated revenue.

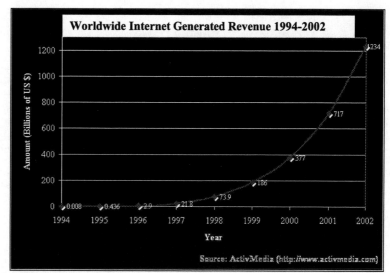

Source: ActivMedia

One of the great disadvantages of the Internet and the Information Society which some pundits are claiming it is creating, is that there is a growing distinction between the 'haves' and the 'have nots'. The geographical location where the Internet has made the greatest impact is in the United States. In 1998, 57% of the online population were in North America, with Europe at almost one-third of this figure with 21.75%. Businesses in the real world still have to worry about geographical location, about shipping costs and about their target audience. Whilst it is wonderful to talk about the global scope of the Internet, in reality this is unlikely to be the case for many years. The Internet, despite its ethos that all should be able to get online, is riddled with inequality. Some less developed areas of the world, such as Africa, do not yet possess a developed enough telecommunications structure to host the Internet. The following table illustrates the number of individuals who currently have access to the Internet.

Geographical Location	No. People Online (millions)	Survey Date	Source
United States	95.8	April 1999	Nielsen Net Ratings
Japan	14.0	October 1998	Nikkei Market Access Survey
United Kingdom	10.6	December 1998	NOP Research Group
Germany	8.4	March 1999	GfK
Canada	7.6	January 1999	ComQUEST Research
Australia	4.4	December 1998	Computer Industry Almanac
China	4	July 1999	International Data Corp.
Sweden	3.6	May 1999	Business Arena, Stockholm
Brazil	3.5	November 1998	Brazilian ISC
South Korea	3.1	January 1999	National Computerisation Industry
Taiwan	3.0	January 1999	Inst. for Information Industry, Taiwan

Geographical Location	No. People Online (millions)	Survey Date	Source
Spain	2.8	March 1999	AIMC
Latin America (except Brazil)	2.2	December 1998	IDC
Africa	1.14	January 1999	SANGOnet
Rest of World	7.16	May 1999	NUA Internet Studies

Notice the current dominance of North America followed by Europe and Japan. However, other regions are catching up fast. In Asia, the number of Internet users is growing exponentially, primarily driven by China. In 1997 China had just 640,000 users. From the above chart, it can be seen that this has grown to 4 million and is expected to rise to 27 million by 2001 (estimates by International Data Corp.). It would be reasonable to assume that in the longer term Asia might well have more Internet users than the USA.

Even within developed countries, the Internet has not achieved majority penetration and is still considered as something for the more prosperous members of society. In the States, only 19% of households whose annual income is under $50,000 are online. However for those earning in excess of $100,000, over 65% are online. Another factor to consider is the age of those online. In the US, 35.5% of adults are online, whereas only 21% of teens and 12 % of seniors are using the Internet. Traditionally computing has been seen as a male dominated field. This is also true of the Internet with well over twice as many men using the Internet as women in 1998, according to NUA Internet Surveys. However, the expectation is that the Internet will become a tool equally used by both sexes. In demographic terms, consumer take-up of the Internet today must be realistically considered by those who intend to become involved in e-commerce. The next chart illustrates Forrester Research's predictions for the growth of e-commerce in the United States.

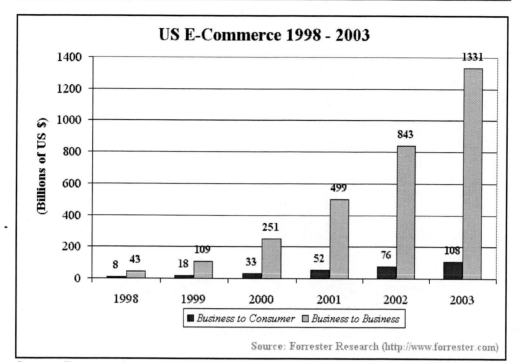

Source: Forrester Research

Note that business to business e-commerce in the US far outranks that of consumer spending online. However, consumer spending is significant. The following chart is taken from a survey by the Graphics, Visualization & Usability Center of Georgia Institute of Technology. The survey was conducted worldwide online in October 1998. The chart shows which products are being purchased online most frequently. It can be seen that travel is second only to computer hardware/software, books and music.

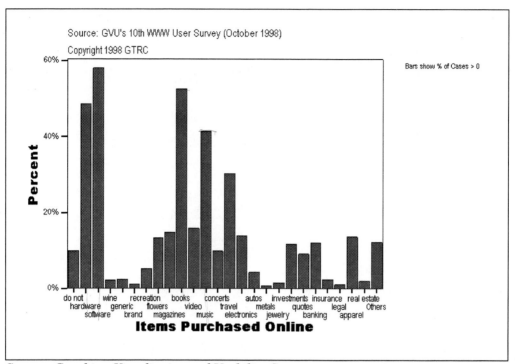

Source: Graphics, Visualization and Usability Center

From the charts and figures in this report, it is clear that the United States currently dominates the online population. This situation, however, can only be temporary. The likelihood is that over the next few years the rest of the world, and in particular the main outbound travel markets such as Europe and Japan, will catch up with the United States. Take-up of the Internet outside of the United States is now mirroring the adoption level which they have been enjoying for the past few years. Analysts consider that from 2000 onwards consumer Internet take-up will rise exponentially in Europe, much as it has been doing in North America since 1996. Along with this, consumer spending through the Internet in Europe will also rise as the adoption brings with it a greater sense of familiarity with e-commerce. The next chart illustrates the projected rise in consumer spending in Europe.

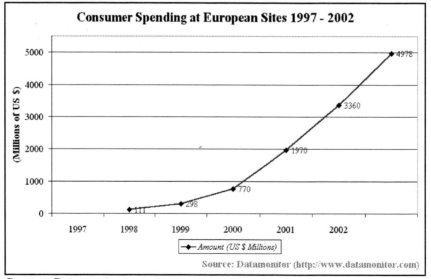

Source: Datamonitor

By considering the growth in the acceptance of the Internet within mainstream consumer society, it is clear that we are just entering a period where the World Wide Web is surpassing its teething stage and reaching early maturity. Although it might be difficult to argue that it has yet achieved universal market penetration, much as television has done, it is even harder to argue that these levels will not be achieved in time. In advertising and in the media, the Internet has been embraced as a new distribution channel by which to reach the general public. Two of the greatest concerns now for the Internet community are political regulation and public attitudes. The graph below indicates that these are the issues within Europe which will continue to hamper a greater consumer take-up of the Internet, rather than just purely technological concerns.

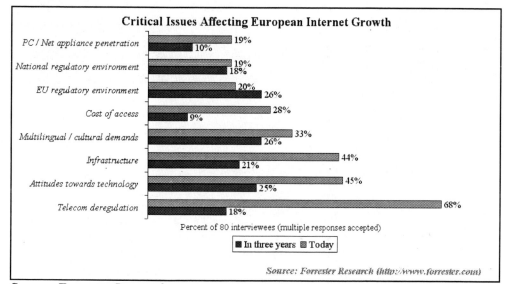

Source: Forrester Research

However what is clear is that these boundaries are being met and broken, and that a time where the consumer take-up of the Internet is comparable with the level of penetration of television is not far off. Consumers are starting to show a preference for surfing the Web over other activities. The last chart in this section, shown on the next page, is also taken from the October 1998 Graphic, Visualization and Usability Center worldwide online survey. It illustrates the response to a question, "Frequency of using the Web instead of .....". It is clear that the Internet is changing society and its social norms.

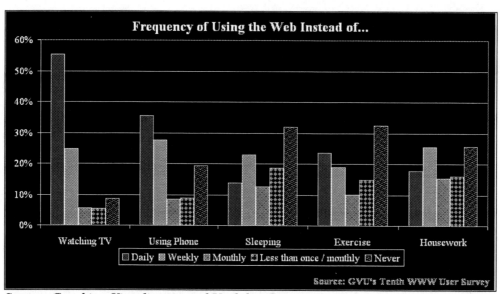

Source: Graphics, Visualization and Usability Center

OTHER CURRENT ONLINE TECHNOLOGIES

It is often assumed that the Internet is the domain of the PC, that without a PC, people are not able to access the Internet and the Web. This was certainly true in past years when the Internet was in its infancy but this situation is now changing fast. There is a range of new technologies that are providing access to the Internet and other online channels. These are set to provide mass online access at affordable prices. It will no longer be necessary to purchase an expensive PC to participate online. For tourism organizations, this means that far more potential tourists will be seeking destination information online.

This move away from use of a PC started with the introduction of Web TV. This is a small "set-top" box connected to a television and a telephone line, allowing users to surf the Web from their televisions. As part of the deal, the user enters into a subscription agreement with Web TV who provides Internet access. Web TV is, in effect, an Internet Service Provider. This was the first Net Appliance, introduced before the term "Net Appliance" was coined as the generic name for Internet connectivity devices.

Web TV made apparent the limitations of surfing the Web on a television. Web sites are designed to be viewed from a PC screen. A PC screen has a higher resolution than a television (ie. the picture has more detail) and is typically positioned about a half metre away from the viewer. A television, on the other hand, is usually placed on the other side of a room from the viewer and may be three or four metres away.

This difference has been recognised by television companies who are introducing Interactive Digital Television (IDTV) services. The screens they are designing in support of their interactive services are bolder in design than Web screens. They have less detail and use larger fonts.

Notwithstanding this, the IDTV companies are planning to provide access to the Internet and the Web. This may lead to the need for Web site developers to produce two versions of their sites, one for PC viewing and one for TV viewing. The technologies of IDTV, net appliances and e-ticketing, all of which will encourage and facilitate the online purchase of travel and tourism, are now reviewed.

Interactive Digital Television

Within the United States and Europe over the past couple of years, we have seen the rollout of interactive digital television (IDTV) services, hastening the move into the Information Age. Digital television extends televisions communication power by providing interactivity. Digital television means that computers and TV now speak the same language. The same principles used to bring moving pictures to a computer screen, such as on a CD-ROM encyclopaedia, are used to bring digital television to our screens.

What is Digital Television?

The traditional method of broadcasting television pictures has been by use of analogue signals. Analogue signals are exact representations of the original information (in this case sound and picture). Digital signals do not operate in this manner. They operate in binary form, just as a computer does. The television signal is converted to an encoded representation and transmitted. At the receiver the set-top box interprets that signal and converts it to a television image. The signal which arrives is not the exact representation of the sound and picture, it is an encoded representation. Effectively the set-top box is a computer. Its input is binary information, it processes it and outputs it to the television just as a computer would.

As illustrated on the next page, there are three types of technology, each incompatible, each with their own qualities, each with their particular advantages and disadvantages.

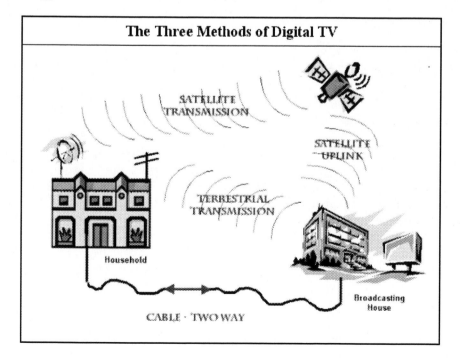

35

Digital Satellite is exemplified by SkyDigital in the United Kingdom. Sky's analogue service has dominated the British paying television service for years. It has an established client base and is a household name. During the back-end of 1998, it released its digital service, SkyDigital, based around its existing methods of transmission, through a satellite dish. Because SkyDigital uses satellites for transmission, it has a huge amount of bandwidth to utilise and therefore can broadcast a very large number of channels. Technologically SkyDigital is not a two-way interactive service. Whilst digital signals can be transmitted from the satellite, there is no way that the receivers can send information the other way. Therefore, subscribers are being offered large discounts to connect their set-top boxes to a telephone line.

Digital Terrestrial Television – The signals are broadcast identically to current, traditional, analogue, terrestrial channels, and are received through the same standard television aerial. However they are digital and are received by a set-top box connected to the television. Once again, interactivity is enabled by connection to a telephone line.

Digital Cable – Suggested by some to the best of all the IDTV technologies. The medium is two-way, meaning that information transmitted from the set-top box can be sent back to the source of the transmission along the cable, much like on the Internet. Aside from television, trials are also taking place to use the cable infrastructure to deliver connectivity to the Internet through cable modems. The greatest issue with digital cable is that to set up a cable infrastructure is hugely expensive, so it will only ever be introduced in areas of high urban density.

What is the Potential for Digital Television?

Interactivity, in a word. Interactivity means that viewers can respond and alter the content, on an individual basis, of the television they watch.

Imagine the Internet as it is today. Consumers can:

- Shop online
- Glean information online
- Request video (albeit poor quality video currently) online
- Request music online
- Communicate online.

Imagine television with the same features. This is the potential of interactive digital television. Viewers, instead of going to a travel agent, could request to view information of the destination that interests them. If the viewer wants to buy a holiday, a simple command to the box would send the viewer to the television provider's online e-commerce store.

The chart below illustrates projected take-up of IDTV set-top boxes in Europe.

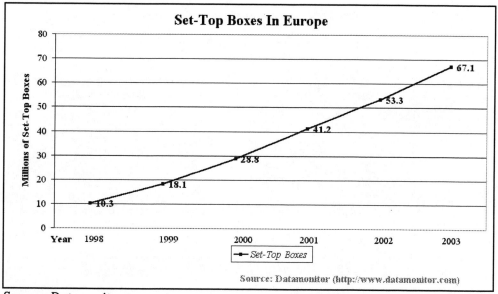

Source: Datamonitor

The Potential for the Travel Industry

From the point of view of the travel and tourism industry, the benefits of this new channel are the provision of destination information and fulfilment of direct sales through e-commerce. IDTV connects the consumer to the Internet (for this is the most likely development of the technology) promising a worldwide audience and fully electronic systems. Ticketing, distribution and payment can all be achieved directly and without manual processing from anywhere in the world. Because of the developments in secure electronic access, there will be reliable means by which to check the identity of the payee and less chance of administrative mistakes.

The technology sounds very similar to that of the Internet and, indeed, it is. The primary differences is that a television is typically located in a consumer's living room whereas a PC is often located in a study or spare bedroom. This means that the TV lends itself to the family viewing that is required when purchasing travel and tourism, just as a printed holiday brochure will be shared viewing across the family.

The chart below illustrates digital TV penetration in Europe by country.

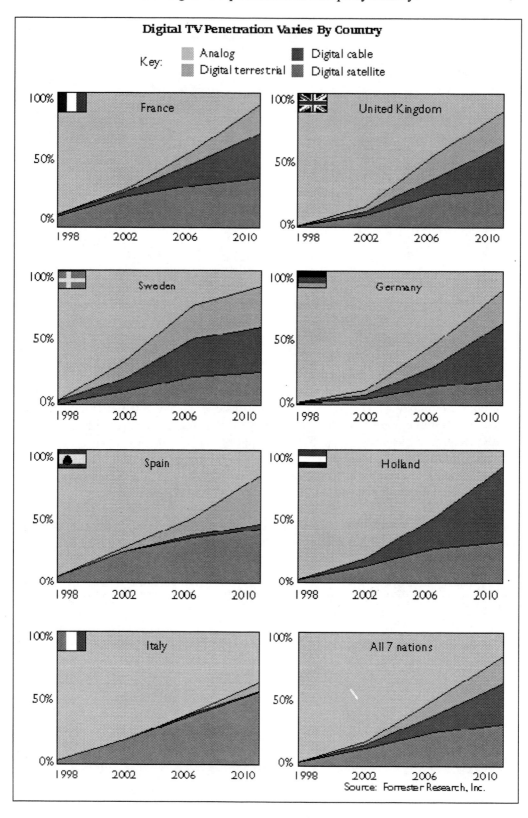

Source: Forrester Research

One of the key considerations for the travel industry is how well this technology will be adopted by consumers. Research into this area suggests that already Internet users feel happy with buying online and this trend will grow. The final, perhaps clinching factor, is that currently Internet marketing and advertising is not as sophisticated as its television counterpart. IDTV will marry the two technologies sufficiently to remove this barrier. Information and sales will not only be accessible, but also more appealing. Brochures may be moving imagery or three dimensional. Updates to bookings databases will be done in real-time. The advances in such technology will bring a level of consumer sophistication that cannot be achieved today.

Why the Potential of IDTV will be Fulfilled

Since 1996 in the States and more recently elsewhere, the level of Internet take-up has been dramatic. Within the next ten years most believe that the Internet has the potential to reach penetration levels comparable to television. Moreover, governments, such as those in Britain and the States, have declared their intentions to turn off analogue transmissions by 2010. There is a real commitment to IDTV.

In 1998, Microsoft bought WebTV for $425million, a company that provides consumers with Internet access via a set-top box connected to a standard television. The direction in which Microsoft is moving is towards enhanced networking, video streaming technologies and advanced Internet usage. Its computer based product strategies are migrating to the multi-media broadcast technologies of television.

Interactive digital television is firmly in the minds of companies such as Microsoft. Whereas currently many e-commerce ventures are losing money, their investors are happy to continue to invest because of the potential for earnings when IDTV becomes a reality.

The next case study is about one organization, ntl, that is pioneering the development and adoption of interactive digital television.

Case Study: ntl

ntl Incorporated, owned by holding parent ntl, is a pioneer of new technologies in telecommunications, TV, radio, Internet and interactive services. ntl is the largest broadband telecommunications provider in the UK and Ireland, as measured by number of customers. Revenue grew from $147.7 million in the first quarter of 1998 to $313.4 million in the first quarter of 1999, against a background of acquisitions in the UK and Ireland, Continental Europe and Australia. International acquisitions have formed the basis for two broad focuses. Firstly, ntl Broadcast, which will concentrate on broadcast infrastructure, particularly national broadcast networks as they are privatised in order to provide funding for digital television, eg. Australian National Transmission Network. The second company focus, based at a state-of-the-art digital media centre in the United Kingdom, will be ntl's drive to build a pan-European cable network based on digital developments in the UK. Steps to achieve this to date include the purchase of CableLink, a cable franchise in Dublin, and the purchase of the 1G networks around Paris.

One million already subscribe to analogue cable TV with a total 1.4 million subscribing to either analogue cable TV or analogue cable telephony. ntl's closest competitors, Telewest and Cable & Wireless, currently hold 24% and 21% respectively of all available UK franchises. By early 1999, ntl had a base of 1.8 million subscribers across analogue cable TV in the UK and Ireland. This represented a five fold increase from the previous year.

ntl's vision is to make life easier for consumers by giving them one number to telephone from where they will be quoted a single price for a package including telephony, Internet access, digital TV, interactive services and, in the future, mobile telephony.

March 1999 saw the launch by ntl of the UK's nationwide first TV based interactive services. Using a set top box, which utilises a land line modem (56kbps), 'TV Internet' offers the prospect of Internet access to 16 million homes across the UK that do not have a PC. In addition, partners provide special content for travel, entertainment, sport, news, local and shopping channels. ntl's mission for its travel content is to make it the primary source of transactions and information for travel within subscribers' homes. At this time, its travel channel includes a wide range of travel products and services which can be directly purchased through the TV set from bargainholidays.com, Travelselect and ABC Traveltime.

The next step will be to roll out a fully fledged interactive service over digital cable in September 1999 and, soon afterwards, a digital terrestrial TV service including interactive services.

Working with key players in each travel and tourism sector, ntl's expanded digital travel channel should provide an easy to use online environment for viewers to research and purchase travel products. ntl believes that the majority of the population do not want to make the time-investment needed to learn how to search and navigate individual Internet sites. It is structuring its travel channel around what the user wants, with the allocation of specific product sections, eg. flights, package holidays and so on. ntl is saving consumers the trouble of going on the Internet or down to the high street to find the right packages at the right prices. Their travel channel will provide the ability to shop around for similar travel products and services from different vendors from the comfort of their own home.

The important difference between platforms (TV, PC, net appliance) is the interface. The data stored on the background e-commerce engine remain the same. Using the Internet's technology standards, ntl envisages linking content directly from partners' e-commerce engines to each ntl platform via ntl's central payment zone. Information can be correspondingly displayed in relation to each ntl platform interface. For example, in the future it will be possible to review the same travel itinerary on an ntl connected personal digital assistant as previously booked over ntl interactive TV.

In the Information Age, there will be nothing to stop viewers from moving between technologies, interactive TV sites and Internet sites. ntl, in partnership with RealMedia, are in a position to provide the first broadband interactive advertising services. Travel and tourism organizations will be able to implement and extend their proposition across all platforms giving viewers the opportunity to directly click through from television to interactive services and make a transaction or request information.

Ian Gosling, ntl Interactive Channel Manager for travel, relates the future impact of interactive TV in the travel industry to the impact ATMs (Automated Teller Machines) had in the banking sector, where simple data entry work became automated leaving fewer counter staff to specialise in more complex financial services. In the context of the travel industry, he believes this will mean a shift in high street travel retailing towards selling more complex quality products while simpler travel transactions move over to the interactive TV environment.

Whilst, ntl provides a digital pipeline to the consumer, it does not itself develop programming. One organization that does this, with a specific focus on travel, is Travel Channel. The next case reviews the issues that face this company tasked with developing programming content purely related to travel and tourism.

Case Study: Travel Channel

Travel Channel broadcasts in the United States and United Kingdom. It is owned by parent company Landmark Communications (US), broadcasting niche programming sixteen hours a day across Europe and Africa through cable and satellite television proviers. Travel Channel also provides programming for UK terrestrial television. While the company derives some revenue through advertising, its primary emphasis is to provide quality content. There are three main content components all related to travel and tourism. Firstly, programmes featuring high profile presenters. Secondly, in-house destination documentaries. The third area includes a mixture of supporting content such as a live phone-ins, weather information and travel news.

The Travel Channel distributes its signal across 20 European countries plus Africa where their potential base is 48 million cable homes and 26 million DTH/SMA TV homes.

Travel Channel's programming has wide international appeal. It is not the intention to dilute content quality in order to provide programming down new channels offered by digital broadcasting. The benefits of digital will be used instead to enhance existing programming. For instance, Travel Channel will move to dedicated UK, European and African channels in the fourth quarter 1999. Over time, certain aspects of the channel will become increasingly localised such as departure information. The immediate strategy is to surround the 'Travel Channel' with two side channels 'Holiday Guide' and 'Holiday Shop'. These are only working titles at the time of writing. Each side channel will be platform independent compatible, with video-on-demand, broadband satellite broadcasting to PC, travel text, and other emerging platforms.

Travel Channel wants to tell cable viewers that there is more to the 'Travel Channel' than just entertaining programmes. It will remain entertaining but also intelligent and useful should the viewer want to plan or buy a holiday. Software for the interactive versions of the Travel Channel is expected in the fourth quarter of 1999. The first layer of interactivity on digital cable and satellite will be invoked either by an on-screen icon or with remote control button, depending on the platform. Pressing this will give the choice of either going into 'Holiday Shop' or 'Holiday Guide'. Once entering 'Holiday Guide' the viewer can then decide to go straight into an editorial database related to the country on air at that time. In most cases the viewer can also choose to keep the programme running in the bottom right corner of the screen.

Worldwide destination information in text and still image format can also be accessed from a menu. Each country has several categories such as 'health and safety', 'getting there', 'spending money', 'future programmes', 'the experts view' and so on. Of course information provided by experts and viewers will not always be positive. Travel Channel is committed to being user friendly and on the side of the viewer.

'Holiday Shop' has been designed to cater to the needs of the commercial players where viewers can search for holidays through an on-screen menu and enjoy all the benefits of digital technology such as downloadable brochures. 'Holiday Shop' looks and feels completely different from 'Holiday Guide' - an interactive content oriented version of Travel Channel. Travel Channel are currently investigating, with the big tour operators, the details of how the transaction process will work. The main problem is that the interfacing software currently used to support viewdata is not yet sufficiently robust to support 'Holiday Shop'. The viewer can search for holidays under different categories including by tour operator, destination, airport, price range and so on. Using the remote control, the viewer can scroll down a screen presented with a mixture of text and images. Although this sounds like Teletext it will be instantly navigable and appear at a much higher resolution thanks to increased bandwidth.

Travel Channel anticipates that consumers seeking travel information will feel more comfortable with 'lean back' TV viewing than 'lean forward' PC viewing. The editorial database, Holiday Guide, is initially generated from material researched for its programmes. Additional material added into the database is also used to support the Travel Channel's Web site. Content includes research into the opinions of holiday makers, historical insights and further related destination information. The opportunity exists for DMOs to provide well grounded destination content. In the past, Travel Channel found they could not always take at face value material provided by DMOs. This underlines the need for more open partnerships which in the future could encompass the channelling of well rounded destination coverage of both the formal and informal tourism sectors.

The challenge of keeping a database up to date in the Information Age is becoming a full time task with features such as video on demand putting viewers in control of what they want to see. Over time, DMOs collating databases as eruditely and honestly as possible are more likely to form partnerships and consequently gain a greater degree of coverage. DMOs located where the Travel Channel does not have full time crews could also stand to capitalise on that position and consider providing more specialist content information in digital format such as mpeg video footage and jpeg still images.

In summary, Travel Channel, whilst positioning as a new travel distribution intermediary, will play an important role in helping to mould viewers' value judgements on destination choice. With those developments taking place outlined above and the opportunities presented by new technologies, the Travel Channel also stands to benefit from the financial backing of corporate parent Landmark Communications (U.S) and the cross unit exploitation of organizational learning e.g. the 'Weather Channel', in-house magazines and radio broadcasting.

Net Appliances

Although the Internet is mostly associated with PCs, there are other methods of connecting to the Internet. These are all potential ways in which consumers can gain access to travel and tourism products. There are several different types of device that will come into common use over the next two or three years.

Network Computers

Although not a new concept, network computers (NCs) are becoming increasingly popular in the business environment. Possessing limited or no internal data drives, these are effectively cut-down PCs. Their data sources are servers connected to the network to which they are attached, and their access is remotely controlled. Users of NCs access travel and tourism on the Web in just the same way as PC users.

Game Consoles

As game consoles have become more sophisticated, there has been a general shift in the gaming community towards greater connectivity. One upshot of this is that the next generation of gaming consoles will provide Internet access through a built-in or add-on modem. Sega's forthcoming console, Dreamcast (due for release in Europe in September 1999), was released in Japan in 1998 allowing access to the Internet. Sony's next generation PlayStation will also allow its users to go online. The major application for these types of machines is to allow gamers around the world to play against each other over the Internet. However as a by-product it will open up the Internet to those who do not already have it, providing a further body of consumers with access to travel and tourism Web sites.

Set-Top boxes

Whilst this technology was examined in more depth earlier in this chapter, it is worth mentioning that already there are products on the market to allow users to access the Internet through their television. Essentially these boxes use the traditional phone – modem type – connection with the television as the 'monitor'.

Mobile Telephone and Computer Units

Already there are mobile phones or handheld computers that allow you to connect to the Internet. Examples of these are Nokia's Communicator series of mobile phones or Hewlett Packard's collection of handheld Jornada PCs. Whilst very capable for collecting e-mail, their screens are not well suited for Internet browsing. However, airlines and other travel vendors are already examining their potential as a medium through which business travellers will be able to check, make and amend their travel reservations.

Screen Telephones

These devices combine a telephone with a screen to provide Internet capability. Their greatest advantage is that they are permanently on, and so can connect instantly. Their potential audience are those users who already use online systems (such as the French Minitel system) and wish to migrate to the Internet. Minitel has been very successful with around 13 million subscribers.

The chart below illustrates Jupiter Communications' estimates of the take-up of different types of net appliance.

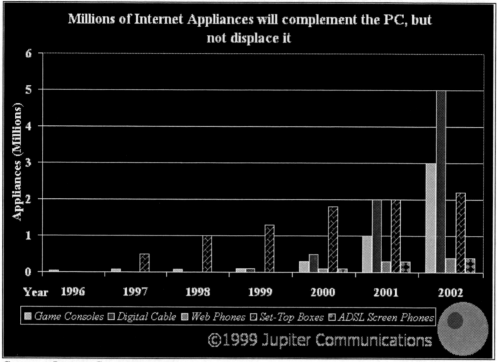

Source: Jupiter Communications

Whilst the above figures seem impressive, it is estimated that Europe's online population will only have increased by 13% as a result of net appliances by 2001.

E-Ticketing

Electronic Ticketing (e-ticketing) is the creation of a ticket, but not as a physical entity. There is no flight coupon to hand in at check-in, no ATB2 (the automated boarding pass and ticket) and nothing to send to the passenger. Whilst nothing is physically produced, the processing and administration automated by a GDS or reservation system is exactly the same as if a ticket had been printed and presented. The travellers identity can be checked through an ID number, passport or credit card when they check-in. The advantages of this type of system are in reduced costs, less administration, heightened convenience and a reduced margin for error.

Developments in e-ticketing will be crucial to the acceptance of online booking systems for direct sales systems and travel agents that exist only on the Internet. Travel agents with such a system could sell from anywhere in the world to anywhere in the world and most of the administration will be done automatically or by the prospect client by entering his/her details into the system. Once a client has booked the ticket, either online or through an agent, the booking is created on the ticketing database for the airline and the passenger receives a receipt and itinerary. The details are sent to the payments and settlements system for processing – in the US this is the Airlines Reporting Corporation (ARC); the other system used internationally is the Bank Settlement Plan (BSP). At check-in the passenger is provided with a boarding pass from the details on the airline database. This system incurs far less administration or delays than any current paper based ticketing system.

Acceptance of such a system might be hard to obtain from passengers and travel agents however. The physical presence of a ticket is very reassuring to travellers and many would be reticent to travel without the comfort of having a physical ticket within their possession. However, with education about the benefits of this type of system, this obstacle may be a relatively easy one to overcome.

Travel agents might object to e-ticketing because it threatens to make them obsolete. With no physical ticket to hand over, there is no reason for the traveller to visit an agent. If this system creates scope for direct sales with no administration or processing overheads, travel agents will see it as a threat to their businesses. Nevertheless, some airlines are now investing heavily in the systems required to administer e-ticketing. It is the final piece in the jigsaw of providing travellers with a completely electronic system of travel bookings. It promises to facilitate online bookings through global networks such as the Internet.

Case Study: United Airlines

Among the first airlines to embrace electronic ticketing (e-ticketing) was United Airlines. From late 1994 the airline was trialling e-tickets on United Shuttle services on the West Coast of America. So successful was this scheme that in mid-1995 United expanded the service. By the Autumn of that year, e-ticketing was being used on all United flights within the US, and between the US and Puerto Rico. Although initially bookings could only be made with the airline directly, by June 1996 this service was available through all the GDSs within the United States.

The programme progressed to include flights between the US and the UK by the end of 1997, making United the first airline to use this technology on transatlantic routes. The plan has been to increase the number of e-ticketed services and by December 1998, United Airlines has been allowing the purchase of e-tickets for transpacific flights, and to many other destinations including, the Netherlands, France, Belgium, Korea, Taiwan, Japan and more. The expectation is that eventually e-ticketing will be the standard used to encompass every GDS booked flight worldwide. United now believes that this service is available across 88% of its worldwide market. The chart on the next page illustrates the rise in the number of e-tickets issued by the airline.

A further progression in this project is allowing e-tickets to be used for more than one flight on a single ticket, for more than a single airline (interlining). Currently United allows for up to 16 flights on a single ticket available over the GDSs from agents or direct from United Airlines in the US, the UK, Canada and Australia. There are a great many advantages to such a system, and United believes that these benefits for the users have outweighed the issue of introducing a new technology to their customers.

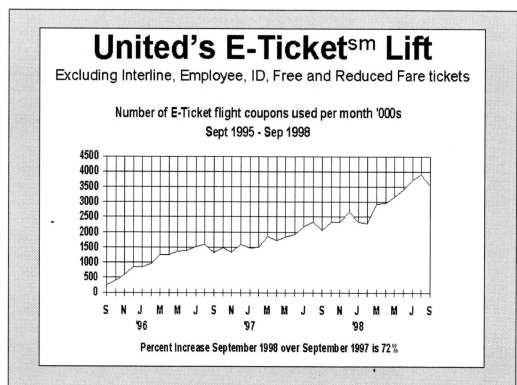

United's E-Ticket^{sm} Lift

Excluding Interline, Employee, ID, Free and Reduced Fare tickets

Number of E-Ticket flight coupons used per month '000s
Sept 1995 - Sep 1998

Percent Increase September 1998 over September 1997 is 72%

However a fuller implementation of interlined e-tickets will rely upon several key issues, most of which concern how each airline will partner another. Payment is a crucial factor and an interlined system would need to be facilitated by the Bank Settlement Plan (BSP) and Airlines Reporting Corporation (ARC). Whilst the issue is not whether or not GDSs can be implemented for such ticketing, it is how long this will take to implement. Currently, United can deal with these types of tickets on its own systems, yet to distribute tickets booked on other airline systems will be a much harder task.

United Airlines has successfully developed an e-ticketing system which is of greater benefit to its customers. It certainly believes that it has been able to overcome many of the problems associated with implementing e-ticketing, such as consumer or travel agent acceptance of such a system. United's e-ticketing system is a very progressive move, but the airline has proven that a committed approach to such technology can be very successful.

E-ticketing is at least as convenient to the traveller as holding a standard ticket. All required documents (receipts, itineraries, terms and conditions, consumer protection notices and other important information) are available to the traveller, even though there's no paper flight coupon. If seats are available for advance assignment, they can be assigned and this is shown on the itinerary/receipt. The traveller shows his/her itinerary/receipt for customs and immigration clearance. This takes the place of a paper ticket for customs and immigrations purposes. If needed, a duplicate itinerary/receipt is provided by the airline.

CHAPTER 4: TRAVEL AND TOURISM – ONLINE AND ON-SALE

INTRODUCTION

Travel and tourism organizations have been quick to grasp the potential of marketing and selling their products on the Internet. In particular, airlines and hotels have realised that they are selling a global product. In a similar way to destination marketing organizations (DMOs), they bring travellers in from around the world. A hotel in the centre of Bangkok or Buenos Aires will have a very high proportion of guests who have arrived from overseas. National airlines such as South African Airways or Air Mauritius will be selling their flights within very many countries outside their homelands. These businesses, like DMOs, sell their product to a worldwide customer base.

The Internet is ideal for this as it can cost no more to be on sale globally as it does to be on sale locally. This is one of the truly exciting features of the Internet. Whereas DMOs marketing campaign budgets needed to increase in proportion to their geographic coverage (with increasing printing and distribution costs), geography is irrelevant on the Internet. There is no more cost associated with 5 million people from around the world visiting your Web site than with just 500 people visiting from your own country.

Moreover, the World Wide Web is an ideal medium for promoting travel and tourism products. It combines all the full colour appeal of the glossiest paper based brochures but with a fixed "print" or development cost. Paper based marketing literature costs more, the larger the print runs. Within bounds, a Web site costs the same to host whether 10,000 or 100,000 people are visiting.

As previously described, travel and tourism is also an electronic product at the point of sale. When a consumer makes the decision to purchase, the product does not exist. A hotel or airline reservation is a computer based booking for some time in the future. The actual stay at the hotel or the flight are not delivered and consumed until a later date. Similarly with destinations. When a consumer takes the decision to visit a destination, he or she cannot touch it or sample it. The information that led to that decision was just that, information; possibly held within a brochure or guide book or perhaps within a Web site. It is this aspect of travel and tourism, the fact that it can be considered an intangible, electronic product before it is consumed, that makes it so suitable for marketing and selling online.

In this chapter, we review travel and tourism consumers online. How popular is travel and tourism on the Web? Are consumers buying product or just browsing for information? What is the profile of the online consumer? Are they frequent travellers?

The next section looks at private sector travel on the Web. How are individual companies tackling the task of online sales and marketing? This is followed by an examination of the public sector, destination marketing organizations (DMOs); how they are starting to embrace the Internet and the challenges they face.

Finally, this chapter explores the activities of new entrants into the travel and tourism industry. Who are they and why have they entered the market?

TRAVEL AND TOURISM CONSUMERS ONLINE

In 1997, only 37% of travel industry Web sites provided means for online booking (the rest providing information only). By 1998 this figure had more than doubled to 76%. For many consumers, online booking of travel is already the norm and this can only continue to strengthen in the immediate future. The direct selling potential of the Internet not only allows suppliers to reach a global market, but also reduces administration costs. Once operating within an electronic environment, computers rather than humans can handle most of the administration automatically. Those keen to enter the market do so because they can see the success achieved by others, and those already in the online market are investing more to protect their initial market share and stay ahead of the game. The following chart provides an overview of features found on travel and tourism organization Web sites.

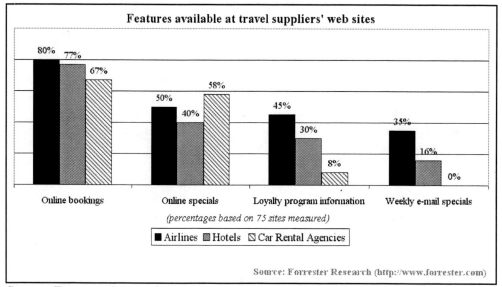

Source: Forrester Research

From the point of view of suppliers it is, therefore, easy to understand why they want to be involved in such technology. Trends in how consumers are shopping for travel online suggest that it is possible to envisage a period very soon when it will be the norm to do so and that to survive, those involved in the travel and tourism industry will need to be involved in direct sales online. There has been some reticence from certain sectors of the industry to tread on the toes of their traditional intermediaries by making the move to direct sales, whilst others have embraced the new online channels with great enthusiasm. The chart below provides estimates of online travel transactions by sector.

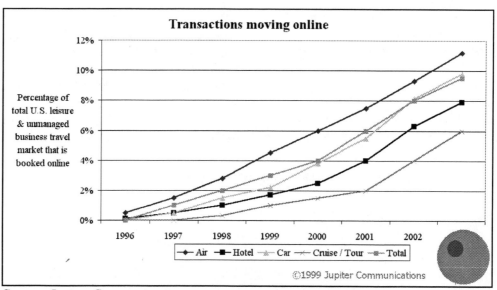

Source: Jupiter Communications

Most travel organizations realise that they need to be on the Internet. The value of online travel sales projected to 2003 in the chart below will be just the beginning. Beyond this, the value of online sales should grow exponentially until it overtakes the revenue from sales via conventional channels.

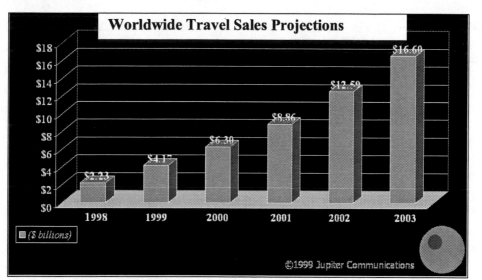

Source: Jupiter Communications

In 1998, over 1 million travel products were purchased online in the United States. Travel is a product that online consumers want to purchase – indeed, according to Forrester Research, it is the product that those who are online, who have not yet purchased online, want to purchase the most. Today's vacation travel consumers are more independent than ever before, meaning that they are happy to hunt around themselves for bargain holidays. There is little need for reliance on traditional travel agencies when it is cheaper, easier and more reliable for those online to use the Internet to book their travel and accommodation.

All projections maintain that air travel holds the largest percentage of online travel and tourism bookings, and that this will remain a dominant feature of travel e-commerce. This is not surprising given the high percentage of United States consumers online. In the US, air travel can be likened to bus travel in smaller countries and, as such, it is a simple purchase. For this reason, the expectations are that airlines will expand their direct online sales programmes in the coming years. Major airlines are expected to add car rental and hotel booking options to their online sales channels, and to allow consumers to create their own packages over the Internet. From 2001 onwards, travel sectors other than air are expected to experience the same levels of growth. The next chart illustrates projected online bookings share in 2003.

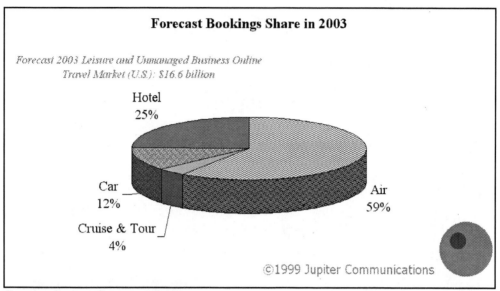

Source: Jupiter Communications

According to Jupiter, direct sales for hotels will not reach the same level as air by 2003. However, it is never easy projecting the future and others, such as Forrester Research, believe that the value of online hotel sales will be much closer to air. Forrester's figures are given in the tables below.

Value of Worldwide Online Leisure Bookings ($ millions)						
	1998	**1999**	**2000**	**2001**	**2002**	**2003**
Airlines	1616	3685	5791	8113	9614	10625
Hotels	1111	2735	4597	6873	8582	9956
Tour Packagers	175	763	2368	3519	4424	4779
Car Rental	171	481	789	1246	1448	1566
Cruise Liners	0	134	405	981	1974	2521
TOTAL	**3073**	**7798**	**13950**	**20732**	**26042**	**29447**

Source: Forrester Research

Number of Leisure Trips Booked Online (millions)						
	1998	**1999**	**2000**	**2001**	**2002**	**2003**
Airlines	2.45	5.50	8.53	11.73	13.70	14.87
Hotels	4.44	10.84	17.97	26.46	32.46	37.12
Tour Packagers	0.13	0.55	1.69	2.47	3.05	3.22
Car Rental	1.14	3.16	5.08	7.89	8.99	9.53
Cruise Lines	0.00	0.05	0.14	0.32	0.64	0.80
TOTAL	**8.16**	**20.10**	**33.41**	**48.87**	**58.84**	**65.54**

Source: Forrester Research

Those concerned with selling online need to understand the current market and how this will develop over the next few years. Presently the majority of those who buy leisure travel online (as opposed to business trips) are young adults with average disposable incomes and who are willing to experiment with buying through this new technology. Their major concern is price and they prefer to travel economically. They are not tied to families and so do not have the responsibility of making travel arrangements for others. For this type of person, the Web offers a freedom from buying conventionally through travel agents. Purchasing online is exciting and new.

Of those who have families or who are older, their larger incomes make them more likely to have access to the Web. However, this is not to suggest that they frequently buy online. According to Forrester Research, these groups are more likely to use travel agents and more traditional means of purchasing travel. They are also likely to spend more on travel than younger adults. This is either due to family holidays, or because they prefer to stay at more expensive resorts or hotels. Forrester found that each group accounts for around the same level of online spending, the younger travellers being lower spenders but booking online more frequently, the more mature travellers booking online less yet spending more when doing so.

As we move further into the Information Age and all segments of the population become comfortable with booking online, the figures will probably revert to their traditional norms.

Browsing Travel Web Sites

NPD Research surveyed 6,000 people during summer 1998 and found that 70 percent of Web surfers have visited a travel related site. Of those that said they had visited a travel site, 80 percent said they had visited airline sites.

The study found that the amount of traffic to travel related Web sites had doubled since a survey in 1996. The number of people going to car rental sites, hotel sites, Expedia.com and ITN.com has tripled in 18 months.

Half of those polled said they had gone online to check travel rates and of those, nearly 50 percent went on to buy tickets online. The ease of checking airline rates online is a large factor in the surge of traffic to travel Web sites over the last year.

Surprisingly the survey found that only 10 percent of those surveyed said they would be extremely or very likely to avail themselves of a discount package in the next 6 months. The survey found that the average visitor to a travel related site was wealthy with an average salary of $60,000 and aged between 24 and 54. Males are slightly more likely to visit airline sites than females.

Online Travel Industry – 1998 Figures

6.7 million US adults used the Internet to make a travel reservation in 1998, up from 5.4 million in 1997, according to a report by the Travel Industry Association of America, TIA.

The 'Technology and Travel 1998' report is based on a telephone survey of 1,200 US adults, conducted during September 1998. Online reservations were classed as those where the consumer used the Internet to book or pay for such things as tickets, hotel rooms, rental cars, and package tours.

In 1998, 33.8 million US adults used the Internet for general travel planning, according to the report, compared with 11.7 million in 1997 and 3.1 million in 1996. TIA found that 45 percent of US Internet users were frequent travellers, making five or more trips during 1998. 92 percent travelled at least 100 miles from home last year.

European Online Travel Industry to Boom

The European online travel industry is expected to generate $1.7 billion in sales by 2002, up from $7.7 million in 1997, according to a report by Datamonitor.

Currently, the most developed and lucrative sector of the online travel market is flight sales. However, online package holiday sales are expected to grow substantially in the future. The advent of interactive TV over the next five years is also expected to be a major boost to online travel sales, according to the report. The study also found that the cost of making a transactional booking online can be up to ten times less expensive than making such a booking through a call centre, an added incentive for would be online consumers.

Europe's Teletext culture, that of buying late availability travel flights and packages as advertised on the service, is likely to make the transition to online purchasing easier for many European consumers, according to the report. The increasing sophistication of travel Web sites, and the convenience of buying online, is also likely to entice consumers to purchase electronically.

Online Hotel Bookings

Online hotel bookings are expected to generate $3.1 billion by 2002, accounting for a quarter of the overall Internet travel industry revenue, according to a report by Bear,

Stearns & Co, the investment bank. In 1997, online hotel bookings accounted for $100 million, representing just 9 percent of the total revenue.

The survey estimates that in 1998 there were about 150 million visits to Web sites that offered a hotel reservation service. The number of visits to these sites is expected to triple in the next four years.

PRIVATE SECTOR TRAVEL ON THE WEB

Private sector travel companies are participating on the Web in their thousands. They have recognised that this is a cost effective channel of distribution that can enable them to reach out to their customers around the world. Listed below are the sub-directories within the commercial travel companies section of Yahoo!, the Web's most successful search directory. The figure alongside some of the names is the number of entries within that sub-directory. For example, Yahoo! lists 28,586 lodgings, 591 airlines.

It should be borne in mind that Yahoo!'s editors are selective about which Web sites are included within its pages. There are actually far more travel related sites on the Web than are listed by Yahoo!. Whilst it would be impossible to count the number of travel related sites, a reasonable estimate would be as many as 250,000.

/Recreation/Travel/By_Region/	/Business_and_Economy/Companies/Sex/Adult_Services/Travel/
Agents (1336)	Airlines (591)
Airports (313)	/Business_and_Economy/Companies/Transportation/Aviation/Aircraft/Airships/
Auctions (5)	/Business_and_Economy/Companies/Books/Shopping_and_Services/Booksellers/Travel/
/Business_and_Economy/Companies/Transportation/Buses/Bus_Lines/	/Business_and_Economy/Companies/Automotive/Rentals/
Concierge_Services (18)	Conferences (10)
Consulting (42)	Cruises (431)
/Business_and_Economy/Companies/Hospitality_Industry/Event_Planning/Corporate_Events/Destination_Management/	Directories (74)
Disabilities (45)	Frequent_Travel_Programs (14)
/Business_and_Economy/Companies/Health/Travel/	/Business_and_Economy/Companies/Travel/Lodging/Hotels/
Incentive_Travel (35)	/Business_and_Economy/Companies/Financial_Services/Insurance/Travel/
/Business_and_Economy/Companies/Automotive/International_Driving_Permits/	/Recreation/Travel/Jewish/
Lesbian__Gay_and_Bisexual (14)	/Business_and_Economy/Companies/Transportation/Limousines_and_Shuttles/
Lodging (28586)	Luggage_and_Accessories (264)
/Recreation/Travel/News_and_Media/Magazines/	Membership_Clubs (39)

Newsletters (10)	Organizations (46)
Passport_Services (19)	/Business_and_Economy/Companies/Publishing/Travel/
/Business_and_Economy/Companies/Travel/Lodging/Resorts/	/Business_and_Economy/Companies/Food/Restaurants/
/Business_and_Economy/Companies/Outdoors/Camping/RV_Parks_and_Campgrounds/	Software (79)
Tour_Operators (4855)	Trade_Magazines (6)
/Business_and_Economy/Transportation/Trains_and_Railroads/	/Business_and_Economy/Companies/Transportation/Trucks/Trucking/Truck_Stops/
Videos (36)	Vocational_Schools (24)
Women (3)	

Source: Yahoo!

Marketing and distribution on the Web is best suited to those travel companies that offer a product that is on-sale globally and is sold to consumers that are confident users of the Internet. Consider the following diagram:

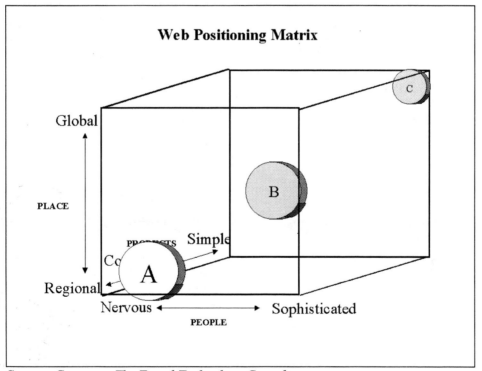

Source: Genesys – The Travel Technology Consultancy

The Web Positioning Matrix is a three dimensional representation of marketing space on the Web. The three dimensions are:

1. People – ranging from sophisticated consumers, who are familiar with using the Internet and who are also frequent travellers, to nervous consumers who would be reticent to buy travel on the Web as they use the medium infrequently and perhaps travel just once or twice per year.

2. Product – describing a company's travel product that may range from being simple, such as a hotel room or a return flight, to complex, such as a multi-leg tour.

3. Place – a characteristic of the product. Is it an inbound product that can be sold globally? Examples are an inbound ground handlers products or hotel accommodation in an international destination. At the other end of the spectrum, does the product have regional characteristics? Is it, for example, a holiday package with flights operating from a regional airport?

Utilising these three dimensions, it is possible to position travel organizations within the matrix. The diagram shows three hypothetical companies, A, B and C. Company A may be a small tour operator selling package holidays with flights out of a small regional, airport. Positioned in the bottom left hand corner of the matrix, illustrates that it has the least market potential to sell products on the Web. Company B is floating in the middle whilst Company C is the organization that is most likely to gain substantial revenues through trading on the Web.

Company C may be, for example, a national airline. Its product is global as its routes bring passengers into its own country. It may be targeting business travellers who are sophisticated users of the Internet and feel comfortable with purchasing online. The product that it is primarily selling is return flights, a concept that is simple and easily understood. Organizations such as Company C should be investing heavily in having a presence on the Web with full e-commerce facilities that allow visitors to the site to check product availability and purchase online with a credit card.

Whilst Company C type organizations will thrive on the Internet, all categories of travel company are now represented, as can be seen from the Yahoo! listing. A cross-section of these are reviewed as case studies in this section:

- American Express – a large travel agency with a global reputation

- STA Travel – another international intermediary specialized in student travel

- Sportscar Tours – a small incoming tour operator with a niche product

- Kuoni – a large tour operator specialising in long haul destinations

- Forte Hotels – a global hotel chain.

Each is faced with a different set of challenges to successfully distribute on the Web, the issues to be tackled being particular to their type of company and product characteristics.

The first case study concerns American Express, a travel agency with a worldwide reputation. It has a clear strategy of harnessing advanced technology to maintain competitive advantage.

Case Study: American Express

American Express Company (Amex) was founded in 1915. Today it has three core groups including Amex Financial Advisors, Travel Related Services and Amex Bank.

In 1982 Travel Related Services recognised that it was uniquely positioned to compete against other business travel agencies by offering a comprehensive set of services to help manage company travel and entertainment spending. These two functions were combined into a sub-division - Travel Management Services - now known as Corporate Services.

After a period of consolidation in the industry during the eighties, Corporate Services went on to set many of the major trends in business travel management during the 1990s including; global servicing, combined travel and data reporting, management fee/transaction fee contracts, providing consulting services and a range of technological developments.

By mid 1999, Amex was approximately 2_ times larger than its nearest corporate travel competitor.

In 1995, Amex embarked on becoming a major player online driven by the emerging proliferation of Internet usage in business, the movement by agents from commission to fee based arrangements, shortages in travel counsellors and the increasing costs of traditional infrastructure.

A highly qualified management team was put together devoted to try to establish Amex as a leader in corporate travel e-commerce involving its Vice President of Product Development as the architect behind Amex's interactive strategy. This originally involved pioneering work, implementing one of the first e-mail based expense reporting systems and e-mail based reservation systems which officially took the first agency booking in December 1995 before the Internet was in general use.

As the Web became viewed as a viable corporate networking platform, Amex formed a strategic alliance with Microsoft in July 1996 to integrate its in-house developed products with a new revolutionary corporate online booking system, AXI TRAVEL (American Express Interactive). This marked a turning point in commitment by large companies towards travel e-commerce travel booking systems. This system processed its first booking in July 1997 and was tested by 20 companies from July to March 1998, when it was officially made available to Amex's entire client base. The time taken to develop and tailor AXI TRAVEL tied in well with the time needed by the corporates to form their own strategy towards implementing AXI TRAVEL. Amex's initiative started to pay dividends at this point with the signing up of new corporate customers.

By mid 1999, Amex had 240 AXI TRAVEL client sites. AXI TRAVEL had achieved this take-up by meeting the needs of several customer groups including corporate business executives, corporate travel managers, corporate travellers, information officers and travel suppliers. Corporate travel managers held sway over whether to take on the system while corporate travellers would ultimately determine whether AXI TRAVEL saved companies' money.

Amex set out from the very beginning to build-in the necessary flexibility for each of those customer groups. This included satisfying corporate travel managers, who initially saw AXI TRAVEL as a threat, designing AXI TRAVEL to integrate seamlessly with their operations. For example, travel managers could implement travel policy by directly entering negotiated fares, preferred suppliers and selected information links. At the same time AXI TRAVEL helped corporate travellers, who had always opted for the most convenient flight times over the phone, to adjust their time of travel according to significant savings clearly seen on-screen. This has enabled travellers to reduce their travel expenditure by an average of 20%. On top of those savings, companies were also finding they could reduce their administrative costs because Amex could lower transaction fees well below those incurred through telephone bookings.

Getting corporate travellers to use AXI TRAVEL turned out to be the toughest challenge. Amex found business travel agencies gave their clients high levels of service. Consequently the motivation for travellers to use interactive technologies was relatively low. There were two reasons for this. Firstly, corporate travellers tended to ask their assistants to call the travel office which normally responded within 20 seconds and secondly, corporate travellers booking themselves, usually had a strong relationship with an individual agent.

In response to this, Amex focused on creating traveller benefits unique to AXI TRAVEL. Value added features included a seat planner, travel directions, a regular traveller template, visa and passport planning tools and customer profiling. Customised seat maps made the greatest impact, recalls Siemborski. "For the first time corporate travellers felt they were personally benefiting from AXI TRAVEL in a way they could not usually do when booking over the phone. Furthermore, travellers found they could create their own profile including frequent flyer numbers, elite statuses, meal preferences, seat preferences and so on." AXI TRAVEL could not only get them the lowest rate through their company's preferred supplier but it could then automatically go to their personal preferences and optimise the reservation accordingly. The regular traveller template also helped to reduce time taken organising regular business trips. All the individual had to do was bring up the appropriate stored trip, change the dates and book it. Those innovations created a major shift in the way corporate travellers booked travel. AXI TRAVEL experienced a month on month doubling of ticket sales during the first half of 1999.

In summary, Amex has achieved competitive advantage on two counts. Firstly CSI planned from the very start to build into AXI TRAVEL the flexibility needed by corporate clients anywhere in the world. Multinationals needed a global solution. Meticulous scenario planning was used with the involvement of European expertise as early as 1995 to ensure AXI TRAVEL would be readily adaptable to international markets. According to research, business travel needs tended to be consistent throughout the world while the business rules differ eg. taxes, date formats, privacy laws and fare rules. During mid-1999, AXI TRAVEL was under beta testing in the United Kingdom before a planned roll out across Europe and into Australia.

On the second count Amex has gained competitive advantage through already having a user base in the US. Corporations considering a new solution had the opportunity to see AXI TRAVEL's successful deployment. Amex had also already demonstrated AXI TRAVEL's capacity to work with new emerging technologies such as voice recognition, personal digital assistant/mobile phone devices and smart cards. This lead has enabled Amex to integrate AXI TRAVEL into new e-purchasing solutions, otherwise known as maintenance and repair operations (MRO) which will become common place in the new millennium. American Express believes that there are no fixed rules in the online environment. Amex's travel operations attributes its ongoing success to its ability to continually refocus.

The next case study concerns, STA Travel, which like American Express is an intermediary, but otherwise a very different type of business, specialising in student travel. It has been quick to realise that students, more than any other sector of the population, have access to the Internet. It has, therefore, specialised in meeting their particular travel needs and has recognised that, in many markets, students are provided with free access to the Internet.

Case Study: STA Travel

Established in 1979 STA Travel Group (Edward Keller Holdings Ltd, Switzerland) is the leading travel agency in the international youth market of the late 1990s. The group has 12 divisions providing representation in 48 countries, including a network of over 200 branches. From 1980 group sales of $12 million dollars the company had reached sales in excess of one billion dollars by mid 1999. The UK Division is the number one performing division by some considerable margin and is the focus of this case study. Much of what is happening in the United Kingdom can be related to the international online strategy.

STA's online strategy first emerged in the US where reactionary moves were made, in the face of competition from the online travel agencies such as ITN, Preview and Expedia, to implement an online booking engine in March 1998. Developed by IXL (San Francisco) this booking engine is being initially anglicised and improved for the UK and Australian markets. IXL is in the process of completely internationalising the engine so that consumers will be automatically redirected to sites reflecting their country of origin.

The STA Travel Group worldwide has an eight person team dedicated to e-commerce. That team includes Dr Adam Dodsworth recruited in the UK to form and implement an online strategy. Dodsworth recognised STA UK needed to make three key moves. The first step was to form a dedicated e-commerce department with a motivated Internet trained and Internet literate sales team. Secondly, to get the booking engine in place and the early development programme up and running. The third step was to go out and start talking with potential partners. Dodsworth had no doubt that STA could potentially become the biggest online travel seller in the European youth market given its existing competencies in that sector.

STA UK is well integrated into the UK academic network with campus branches, strong relationships with student unions, academic departments and the wider education system. There are approximately 4.5 million students in the UK of whom 125,000, during 98/99, had booked travel through STA. Significantly only STA and Campus Travel offer student fares. Competitors, including new online intermediaries, charge for making alterations to round the world itineraries. As an international company STA has been able to go out to the airlines and save them money and time by taking care of alternations once the flight is booked. In most cases students can go into any branch of STA and change their tickets free of charge. STA also stands to benefit from the education systems drive to support students with online facilities. Students are seen as an important early adopting market of online services. Furthermore students benefit from the incentive of free access to the Internet. STA considers itself to be the leading interface between the student market and the travel industry.

Whilst still in the first phase of formulating a strategy, STA UK saw visitors to its Web site triple over the three months April to June 1999. Telephone sales originated through the Internet had also mirrored independent growth forecasts for online travel sales.

In many cases existing partnerships have been pursued online. In the medium term STA UK expects to work with Student UK (UCAS), a new ISP dedicated to students due to be launched during 2000. Other potential partners might include computer retailers, mobile phone companies and at the top of the list. a major credit card company. On the destination information side, STA is already working with World Travel Guides to integrate content. Interest has also been expressed in working with DMOs, for example, through online promotions such as free flights to Australia.

In the future Dodsworth envisages adding a range of value added features to the site. For example a mobile phone service, supplied by Sabre, allowing users to check the status of their booking. Free e-mail is also under consideration. Integration of online facilities into STA agencies and University locations is another ongoing strategic move. STA already has links with the University of London's computer centre and recently launched a cyber-café in London with another one expected to follow in Liverpool.

The next case study is about Sportscar Tours, a very new business selling a niche product - driving tours in the United Kingdom in Morgan sportscars. The business has been founded with the specific strategy to promote itself on the Web via the search engines and through links with auto-enthusiast Web sites. Its founder has proved that travel and tourism organizations can reap the benefits of marketing on the Web without spending vast sums of money.

Case Study: Sportscar Tours

London Handling was established in 1978 by Stuart Crouch. The company is a successful inbound tour operator, so successful that it was recently acquired by a competitor, JAC Travel.

This left its founder free to pursue other business interests. The idea to team up with long time friend Bill Wykeham of Wykeham's Ltd (London), one of the few dealerships specialising in Britain's popular classic Morgan sports car, had been at the back of Stuart's mind for some time. In 1998, those ideas came to fruition, with the development of the Internet as a viable market place, to combine Bill's charismatic Morgans with a tourism product. After a period of several months promoting and organising the product, setting up the Web site turned out be a quick and easy process. The brunt of the work getting Sportscar Tours off the ground had involved going round trade exhibitions and sending out promotional material. It was on the morning of 20th February 1998 that Stuart received a call from Playboy Magazine in Chicago who went on to run a three quarter page article on the product in August 1998. With a circulation of four and half million, enquires started coming in thick and fast confirming Stuart's convictions about the power of the Internet.

Promotional success did not stop with Playboy. Sportscar Tours have worked with a number of related promotional vehicles including Morgan Cars themselves (which co-operated on the text and photographs), a joint London Tourist Board and Bloomberg promotion (exposure across the financial screens in the US), the Cheltenham regional tourist board (Romantic Road) and the Scottish Tourist Board (STB). A significant proportion of the tour passes through Scotland, which led Sportscar Tours into a marketing partnership with the STB. This relationship has involved funding promotional material such as professional photographs and is expected to further develop with the opportunity to integrate future STB promotions. Both partners have benefited through shared costs and joint promotion, a win/win situation.

As momentum picked up, Sportscar Tours was continually surprised at how the Internet could provide a new framework for business. Morgan enthusiasts started to link to the site and Sportscar Tours now provide a downloadable pack including a purpose made logo. One dedicated member of staff has spent much time searching through the specialist car magazine lists in each country. Many of these magazines have subsequently run promotional pieces and established links. Whilst working with a new medium, much of the work involved has been going back to the older ways of operating.

Future developments are likely to include representation on the VisitBritain Web site (BTA), specialist online magazines and enthusiast sites dedicated to Morgan.

Like Sportscar Tours, Kuoni Travel, the subject of the next case study, is considered to be a niche player, albeit not as specialist. Its product focus is long haul destinations that are perhaps considered to be slightly out of the ordinary. It has, therefore, always sought to provide comprehensive destination information and has built up a considerable database of knowledge. Within the United Kingdom, Kuoni is one of the very first tour operators to offer online bookings on its Web site.

Case Study: Kuoni Travel

Founded by Swiss entrepreneur, Alfred Kuoni, in 1906, the Kuoni group toady dominates the long haul market. In 1998 the company had a turnover of £2.3 billion with subsidiaries in Europe, Asia and India; employed 5,500 staff in 300 offices worldwide; and was active in outbound, incoming and business travel sectors. The group has five key strategic units including Switzerland, UK, Europe, Incoming and Business travel. The UK group is split into three centres of competence, the core Kuoni Tour Operation, the Independent Business Units (IBU's) and the Central Services and Development division.

For thirty years, Kuoni has also led the long haul market in the application of new information technologies. 1988 saw the development and testing of Kudos, a flexible viewdata reservations system for travel agents. In 1992, a fully automated transparent link from Kuoni's computer reservation system to Galileo was achieved, providing ultimate flexibility for holiday customisation and access to last seat availability. During 1993, Kudos was rolled out to Kuoni Italy, Spain and France. 1995 saw the addition of a late availability search, automatically monitoring changes to availability on 5,000 selected Galileo flights, assisting agents to swiftly convert late enquiries into firm bookings.

One of Kuoni's key considerations from the mid nineties was to make these systems as flexible as possible, to not only react to changes in the market but also to implement new Internet technologies. One change in the market included a growing demand by consumers to approach Kuoni direct, either to make a booking or to access further details on previously booked travel arrangements.

Kuoni responded to this by improving and extending the expertise of its call centre staff and by launching an Internet strategy. This initially involved the commitment of resources to Internet development in Kuoni's corporate headquarters located in Zurich, Switzerland, where a five to ten strong team was set up in May 1997. After watching competitors' moves and achieving success with the Swiss site Kuoni committed significant funds towards launching a formal UK Internet strategy in November 1998.

Under the auspices of the Central Services and Development Division, Kuoni's UK team worked towards a marketing strategy of capitalising on the growth in Internet travel commerce. More specifically this has involved addressing the needs of the online travel buyer, who typically has travel experience, would consider shorter holidays and expects best value for money. Whilst maintaining and extending the Kuoni brand, forming a closer relationship with and meeting the needs of those individuals was a priority for Kuoni. Kuoni sought to utilise the Internet to; provide 24 hour simple easy to use access to Kuoni products; lower the costs of servicing a booking both before during and after the transaction; provide continually up to date accurate information; learn more about the consumer; and generate sales.

With these objectives in mind, UK technical Internet development took off, initially involving the re-programming of the IBM AS 400 reservation system. An external agency undertook the Web design contract, while long term partner Online Travel (Switzerland) hosted the site in Geneva. With a total of 300,000 different packages offered over the year, the team focused on making 3,000 of those packages available online.

This decision was in part influenced by scripting and resource constraints. Late availability and millennium departures were subsequently uploaded, including fifty hotels in sixteen of the top producing destinations, within eleven countries, such as Antigua, Barbados, Egypt, Maldives, Hong Kong and Thailand.

The site went live on the 31st December 1998, giving consumers the ability make real time transactions - an industry first. Secure Electronic Transaction (SET) technology, a 128-bit encryption standard from VISA and MasterCard, ensures booking arrangements and payments are completely secure. Searches can be conducted by any combination of destination, price and date. After making a booking, the consumer receives a booking reference and within three days a confirmation invoice. Travel documents are automatically sent out. According to one independent test (Travel Weekly UK), a typical booking can be made within five minutes.

The biggest single booking to date was over £4,000 for four travelling to the Caribbean. It was booked on a Sunday night at around 22:30. Against this background of better than expected growth, the present system has always had, even at the busiest times, 60% free capacity.

Evaluation to date has simply involved analysing how customers communicate over the telephone. In terms of researching what consumers want and the way in which they behave, online research from the Swiss market has been compared with what has been occurring in-house in the UK. Within five months of the site going live, Kuoni had already recognised the need to make improvements by re-launching its booking engine and streamlining information, linking more closely within the site. Rather than providing impersonal 'frequently asked questions' (FAQ), consumers can find answers to specific destination queries in corresponding site zones eg. does the Hotel Sunset have a hair dryer? Or What's the best time to go? Any one page on the site might include information from up to four different places around the world including; live weather information; currency exchange rates; destination images and foreign office advice.

By mid 1999, 40% of the marketing plan had been implemented, involving gaining exposure through free media such as press releases, company literature, search engine registration, Internet service provider links, links with DMOs, shopping malls and related online suppliers. Kuoni does not offer many links out from its site, preferring to keep its site self-contained. However, Kuoni was happy to link to ABTA's site (Association of British Travel Agents) where Kuoni is currently the most popular link. Links with DMOs, eg. Antigua, St Lucia, Egypt, have been borne out of a long history of joint marketing activity. These DMOs stand to benefit by offering visitors to their sites the opportunity to actually book a holiday. This underlines the strategic importance of DMO sites as, not only a source of information, but increasingly a place from where transactions can be made. Registered visitors also receive regular updates on content additions.

Further challenges Kuoni has encountered over the past six months include working in an environment that is constantly changing; recruiting people with the necessary hybrid skills in tourism and e-commerce marketing; maintaining the site; and reassuring consumers over security. In Kuoni's experience, customers spending £1200 online normally want to speak with someone on the telephone at some stage.

One of Kuoni's main unique selling propositions is their ability to offer tailor made flexibility at package tour prices. In the future, the Internet site may have potential to offer this flexibility, but at this time Kuoni has had to restrain holiday offerings to true packages, eg. the flight date cannot be changed prior to departure when booking on the Internet; but what Kuoni is offering on the Internet is the opportunity to fly out on any day to a destination with a range of accommodation options.

Kuoni's immediate enhancement plans include adding new destinations, new hotels and also the facility for clients to actually view their booking online. This will not only be an aid for online bookers but also add further value to consumers who prefer to book through an agent but who wish to simply review their booking by entering a booking reference and invoice number. Apart from adding comfort to the client, this will also help reduce demands on the call centre. By the millennium, with the introduction of an e-commerce server, Kuoni intends to have all of its products online, adding a further 44 destinations and 1,950 hotels.

One of Kuoni's ongoing objectives is to continually maintain onsite information. Creating change to add interest to the site is also an ongoing task, although, with travel, visitors might research one destination one day and then come back and look at another destination the next. Kuoni does, however, wish to improve interactivity with destination products. There is some advanced technology that Kuoni will wish to exploit, such as 360 degree images, online video communication, and moving images. However these technologies can potentially become distracting. It was a policy decision early on to keep the site simple. Visitors need no additional software to view the site. Only as new browser developments become prevalent will Kuoni consider adopting them. At this time, visitor statistics indicate a high percentage of visitors using early versions of browser software. Future options under consideration have included holiday auctions, call back buttons, putting brochures online and uploading extracts from Kuoni's in-house consumer magazine 'World'.

In terms of global coverage, Zurich was the first corporate site to go live followed by the UK. France is due to go live in September 1999, whilst Spain and the Netherlands are also considering doing so. Most of country business units at least have a Web presence. However, putting together a global reservations capability was given considerable thought but ruled out because of the array of different systems in use, a legacy of previous acquisitions.

Kuoni envisages interactive digital television having a longer term impact and intends to participate within it as much as possible, eg. interactive conversations on television-screen, via the telephone, could be possible before the middle of 2000.

The ability to analyse and learn more about customers is also something Kuoni hopes to develop, working towards benefiting from the Internet's most powerful potential - one to one marketing. Those companies who are prepared to grasp the technology and take the opportunity will ultimately benefit the most. One of the benefits of having been at the forefront of new technologies over the past two years will be the ability to apply this knowledge within the context of new emerging channels in the next millennium such as digital TV. However, one of the disadvantages for any pioneer is the inherent insecurity in the market place. Consumers may be unsure if they are getting the best deal. Kuoni looks forward to more competition online, in order to encourage and grow the travel e-commerce market.

Whilst Kuoni Travel is an intermediary - as a tour operator it packages other organizations' products - Forte Hotels, the subject of the next case study, owns its hotels and is selling its own properties. Like many hotel chains, it has embraced the Internet as a core distribution channel. Referring back to the Web Positioning Matrix, Forte Hotels is a Company C type organization that can be expected to thrive online. However, the hotel market is highly competitive and there are inherent challenges in positioning a hotel product such that it is bought in preference to a competitor's.

For hotel chains such as Forte, there are considerable savings to be made by encouraging consumers to book direct. Research organization, Datamonitor, estimates that a reservation taken via a call centre can incur 10 times the overhead cost of a reservation taken via an automated Internet system. Further significant savings are to be made in accepting direct bookings and so cutting out the commissions paid to intermediaries such as the GDSs and travel agents.

Typical intermediary charges for a $160 hotel booking might look like this:

Franchise fee	$5.00
Central reservation fee	$2.00
THISCO fee	$2.00
GDS fee	$7.00
Travel agent commission	$16.00
Total	**£32.00**

Source: Distribution Technology in the Travel Industry
FT Retail & Consumer Publishing

This would compare to a cost of about $1 for receiving a booking directly from a hotel chain's own Web site. Clearly, there are substantial savings to be made by encouraging customers to buy online.

Case Study: Forte Hotels

Forte Hotels' Web strategy first emerged two and half years ago with an Internet site that was designed just to provide information. Against a background of rising interest, including bookings received via email, Forte decided to launch its own global database of hotels linked to the Pegasus TravelWeb.com booking engine. Launched in October 1998, the site had a good start thanks to careful consideration given to search engine linking, co-ordinated exposure on all company print material and good PR coverage. Initial partnerships were also established with airlines, online transaction intermediaries and key DMOs such as the London Tourist Board and British Tourist Authority.

Internationally, Forte has a number of management contracts and franchisees, some of whom have independently marketed their properties online. Whilst maintaining a consistent branded identity is important, Forte has embraced these independent initiatives with the intention of providing more support in the form of guidelines and branding material.

One of the first steps will be to establish a corporate Web ring so that each independent, eg. Meridien Phuket, has a click through into the main Meridien directory site. Forte's own branded sites have also been under progression with Heritage launched in March 1999, London Destination in April 1999, Posthouse in late June 1999 followed by Meridien. Each site is strongly branded with its own look and feel.

Since launch, Forte has received a 20 fold increase in hits and a month on month increase of 50% in bookings. Breaking down reservations between those derived through third parties, eg. TravelWeb.com, and in-house sites has yet to be achieved although developments are underway to move over to a branded booking engine. This will also lessen the likelihood of losing custom to other hotels through TravelWeb.com's own branded site. Despite having restricted access to customer information, handled by the intermediaries, Forte is quite happy with the arrangement as long as the bookings come in.

A number of third parties 'screen scrape' Forte information off the GDS booking engines on to their sites. This content is not always correct although clearly these sites do generate extra bookings. It is hard to tell just how many GDS bookings have come through GDS powered web sites. This difficulty will be in part rectified once a system of placing GDSs indicators on Web derived bookings is put in place, although this will not entirely fix the discrepancy.

After finding that the domains forte.com and forte.co.uk were already registered by the Forte software company, Forte Hotels has taken the precaution of registering domain names related to activities both now and in the future. Earlier in 1999, a competitor used the Forte brands within its meta-tags, attempting to influence the search engines to drive traffic to its site rather than Forte's. Whilst Forte found this flattering at the time, it underlines the importance of online monitoring. In the next financial year Forte wants to deploy resources towards monitoring its presence within the search engines and the prevention of 'search engine terrorism'.

As the largest hotel company in London, Forte has worked closely with the BTA and London Tourist Board where Forte enjoys a significant share of the hotel accommodation section on LondonTown.com (London.com). This site receives approximately 2000 hits/day. Initiatives have also included a millennium project with the London Tourist Board and British Airways, along with additional airline relationships. These include integration with online partnerships and frequent flyer programmes eg. Forte and American Airlines are experimenting with a Forte hotel promotion in AA's weekly e-mail push ('Netsaavers') to AAdvantage card holders. 'Netsaavers' offers special destination deals. British Airways together with Forte organised a 'hop over' package, including a cheap fare and three nights accommodation, which BA actively marketed on the US east coast. BA's online London site received an excellent response, in turn generating additional traffic to Forte over a four week period. Forte has also noticeably benefited from placing individual hotels in the enhanced listings on Expedia. Forte anticipates pursuing further online partnerships.

Forte took the decision to keep destination content slimmed down on the corporate site, featuring those hotels under total ownership eg. Heritage and Post House, while benefiting from the comprehensive blend of destination content found on sites like LondonTown. However, as the Forte branded sites go online, eg. Meridien, Forte would like to work with local tourist boards on maintaining some content. This also applies to those hotels under management contracts or franchises who are able to benefit from access to specialist content within their destination.

Parent company Granada is currently exploring ways in which to market interactive digital TV and perhaps use this as a platform for marketing its leisure interests directly into the living room. Eventually Forte wants to hook up the Forte corporate Web site directly with its own reservation system, although Y2K and Euro compliancy work has taken priority. In the meantime, Forte is happy with Pegasus' TravelWeb.com booking engine which is both robust and reliable. Development efforts that are taking place are solely focused on the feel of the branded sites. Two outside agencies including IS Solutions have been involved with this development. Forte's marketing people are adamant that the brand online must be the same as the brand offline.

DESTINATION MARKETING ORGANIZATIONS, IT AND THE INTERNET

So far in this chapter, we have looked at how consumers are taking to the Internet in their search for information on travel and tourism products. We have also seen how the private sector - commercial organizations – are responding by utilising the Internet as a viable, global distribution channel.

This next section examines how public sector, destination marketing organizations have increasingly turned towards information technology and the Internet in particular, as a cost effective medium for promoting their product, the destination.

Towards the Internet

The Increasing Use of IT by DMOs since the mid-1980s

In contrast to the commercial sector, DMOs have been slow to adopt IT in their operations. There were some early adopters during the 1970s, but generally it was not until the late 1980s, that computer systems started being introduced to enhance DMO publications and information operations and, to a lesser extent, to support reservation services.

During the 1990s, as powerful computing applications became more widely available, DMOs have started to use IT more extensively. Initially this was through self-contained systems designed to support specific areas of operations – for example, tourist information offices, information kiosks and database marketing. Often systems were acquired piecemeal by different departments of a DMO and operated quite independently of each other.

Despite their increasing use of IT, most DMOs did not start considering electronic distribution until the increased public awareness of the Internet in the mid-1990s. Few DMOs contemplated the possibility of working with the GDSs. The electronic distribution that did take place was largely through the commercial online providers, such as Compuserve, AOL and Prodigy.

The Internet– New Opportunities for DMOs

Many DMOs, particularly those in developing countries, have a strong focus on dealing with end consumers. They have developed a high level of interest in the Internet, because of its potential to:

- reach large numbers of consumers worldwide with information and product offers, at relatively low cost

- provide information of greater depth and quality than has been possible through the traditional medium of print

- enable consumers to book quickly and easily

- enable large scale savings on the production and distribution of print.

Despite this potential, most DMOs were not particularly quick off the mark in establishing a sophisticated Web presence. Between 1994 and 1996, many destination sites were established by universities (high on descriptive information, low on product offerings) or by new, usually small, Internet companies (strong on advertising product offerings, low on destination content). Where DMOs did have their own sites, they were often no more than electronic versions of their existing print. There were some notable exceptions – the real market leaders such as Singapore with its interactive online guide.

From 1996 onwards, a lot of DMOs started taking the Web seriously, often recognising the opportunity to use the special features of the new medium – interactivity and multimedia. DMO Web sites multiplied rapidly, with increasing quality of graphics and maps, and the facility to book through a CRS, usually by fax or e-mail. The facility to book online remains the exception rather than the rule.

In the past, many DMOs regarded the Internet as somewhat peripheral and the province of the IT department. This is changing, as increasing numbers recognise that Internet activity should be an integral and important part of its marketing programme.

Towards pro-active use of the Internet by DMOs

Up to the present time, DMO Internet activity has tended to focus on the Web. As DMOs' understanding of the medium has increased, it has been recognised that it is not enough to simply wait for consumers to find their sites and that they must actively promote them. This can be by electronic means – by ensuring that they can be found through the main search engines and through links from other relevant sites; or by promotion through traditional forms of promotion – in the DMOs' own brochures, through advertising, travel media activity, etc. Many of the most popular Internet sites are those that are heavily promoted through traditional methods.

There is another important new marketing opportunity through the Internet – the use of promotions by e-mail, carefully targeted to consumers who have the greatest likelihood of 'buying' the destination. Information technology systems offer the potential to store and access extensive information about past enquirers or customers that can help to identify the best prospects for future promotions – in terms of demographic profile, interests, activities, accommodation preferences, etc. Such customer information can be brought together from different distribution channels – telephone, Web, kiosk, tourist information office – and integrated in a single database.

If appropriate, product offers can be customised to the requirements of specific individuals – implementing the concept of mass-customisation. It is possible also to use agency databases to undertake targeted promotions in a similar way to potential new customers.

The opportunities presented by technology for the implementation of relationship or one-to-one marketing are considerable. However, significant issues of data privacy arise and legislation in different countries may well constrain some of the potential.

DMOs and Internet Commerce

DMOs can design and develop their Internet sites to enable consumers to move quickly and easily from travel planning to making reservations. It is sound business sense for them to do so, in order to close the purchase. The key question is whether the DMO itself should handle the transaction or pass it on to another agency.

Many DMOs, particularly national tourist offices, as publicly funded agencies, do not wish to become directly involved. Regional and local DMOs are often more enthusiastic about engaging in commercial activities, particularly where they are public-private partnership organizations, operating as businesses in their own right. For them, the Internet opens up major new opportunities to sell advance reservations of accommodation, travel, entertainment, events, etc. – and potentially other products such as souvenirs, crafts and speciality foods of the destination, and travel insurance. However, there are important issues relating to international transactions over the Internet, relating particularly to security of payments and liability for the tourism products sold. These must be understood and addressed before such transactions are undertaken. There is also the important operational issue of how available inventory can be accessed to allow immediate confirmation – not easy at the local level, let alone the national level.

For those DMOs that do not wish to become directly involved in transactions, it is sensible for them to offer links from their Web site to sites that do offer reservations. These may be the sites of individual tourism businesses, commercial online reservation businesses or other DMOs. Such links can be provided in return for a fee.

Another scenario is where a DMO has outsourced its reservations operations. Here there should be a seamless link from the DMO site.

Tourism Value Chains, Old and New

Traditionally there have been two, quite distinct sets of value chains linking the tourism product supplier with the end consumer – the commercial chains, mainly involving GDSs and travel agents, and often other intermediaries; and DMO chains. The commercial chains have been strong on transactions and weak on destination information. With the DMO chains, it has been the reverse. Generally, there has been little or no interaction between these sets of value chains.

The advent of the Internet, along with the availability of data in digitised form, may lead to changes in this situation. The Internet provides a universally available network for communication, providing the facility for businesses of different types to exchange information and transactions. Thus it will become increasingly straightforward for players in the different value chains to communicate with each other. For DMOs this means that there will be considerable potential to increase the distribution of their destination information by developing partnerships with commercial operators. There may also be opportunities for DMOs to sell products through commercial intermediaries, but this will require agreement on the commercial terms of the transactions as well as the technical ability to exchange information.

Destination Management Systems – An Overview

An Integrated Approach to the Use of IT

Most DMOs have recognised the key role that IT can play in enhancing the effectiveness of their operations. However, as noted previously, IT systems have generally been implemented on a piecemeal and compartmentalised basis during the late 1980s and early 1990s.

Recently there has been recognition of both the need and the opportunity to change this. The need arises from an increasing awareness of the fundamental importance of maintaining information of the highest quality and integrity; and that this is best achieved through the joint efforts of the different departments, working together. The opportunity is provided by the availability of reasonably priced IT, with office networks (usually now in the form of intranets, using Internet Protocol) and computers on every desk. Data should then become a shared resource.

Thus there is a trend towards integrated DMOs, where the core databases, compiled jointly, support a wide range of functions throughout the organization. The same product database(s) would be used for the Web site, on kiosks, at tourist information offices and call centres and to produce publications. Similarly, the customer database would be compiled and used for all the operations dealing with end consumers.

The term 'Destination Management System' has come into use over recent years to describe the IT infrastructure of a DMO. Different people define Destination Management Systems differently, depending on what their system is designed to do. Thus, for example, some see the customer database and relationship marketing applications as an essential component of a DMS and others do not. Increasingly, however, a DMS is regarded as having to support multiple functions from core databases – ie. it should be the infrastructure for the integrated DMO.

On this basis, the Destination Management System takes on a role of fundamental importance for the DMO. The process of designing and implementing a DMS is a complicated one. There have been many mistakes and some failures in different parts of the world. It is important to learn from the experience of others and to plan with care.

Destination Management Systems and the Internet

Today, when a DMO specifies and implements a DMS; Web and electronic marketing functions should be regarded as essential, integral elements. The Web site should use the product database(s) on an interactive, real-time basis. In other words, when a user requests specific information, this would be drawn from the central database and would be fully up-to-date. In the jargon, the Web pages are created 'on the fly'.

Taking things a stage further, DMSs are being developed now that are fully Web-enabled. In other words, information, reservation and other tourism service functions of the system can be accessed and operated across the Web by defined user groups through an extranet. Thus, for example, tourist information staff could use Web browser software to access the system to provide information and reservations for customers; or a hotelier could access the system to update availability or to obtain latest market intelligence. Through such low cost access the usage of the system can be expanded.

Other applications of an integrated DMS

An integrated DMS should support not only the DMO's Web site, but also a wide range of other promotion, marketing and sales applications, including:

- Design and production of printed material

- Tourist Information Centre services – information and reservations

- Call centre services (information and reservations) plus marketing response and fulfilment

- Kiosks – information and online reservations

- Database marketing through traditional channels (mail, telesales, etc.)

- Leisure marketing contact and activity record management – including liaison with travel media and travel trade contacts

- Interactive TV – multimedia information and online reservations

- Content for CD-ROMs

- Supply of data to third parties – publishers, media including broadcasters, etc.

- Proactive electronic ('Push') marketing, to promote tourism products to targeted consumers, travel trade, conference buyers, intermediaries and the media

- Conference marketing contact/sales management.

In addition, a DMS can also support various other functions, such as:

- Project/event management

- Area or site interpretation for visitors

- Tourism supplier/member liaison/contact management

- Corporate press/pr - news releases, annual reports, etc.

- Research, design and analysis

- Administration and finance

- Performance monitoring and evaluation/MIS

- Office functions, including e-mail, presentations, etc.

The introduction of new IT-based functionality in some or all of these areas will have a major impact on the way any DMO works, calling for a carefully planned programme of change management.

The Strategic Challenge

The advent of the Internet is creating both strategic opportunities and challenges for DMOs. We are seeing the rapid emergence of a major new marketplace for tourism. Over the past two years, the major commercial tourism Web sites have reported a very rapid increases in, not only in the number of visitors to their sites, but also, importantly, in the number and value of transactions. As mentioned previously, companies undertaking research on the Internet market, such as Forrester Research and Jupiter Communications are projecting not only that Internet usage and commerce will continue to grow dramatically, but also that the travel and tourism share of this growing market will show a marked increase. It is clear now that, within a few years, the Internet will become an important medium for travel planning and purchasing, affecting the role of DMOs.

Of equal importance is the fact that this new marketplace allows DMOs to communicate directly and relatively cheaply with end-consumers – and with intermediaries as well. Research shows that, overall, the consumers are affluent and have a high propensity to travel, both for business and leisure. Their leisure travel exemplifies strongly the trends of recent years towards independent travel and special interest holidays and breaks.

Thus the Internet represents an increasingly important marketplace of consumers whose profile matches well the requirements of most, if not all, DMOs. In addition, however, the Internet will be used more and more by travel agents instead of brochures and guides to obtain destination information (generally from bookmarked sites offering quality information on attractions, events, weather, etc.) to back-up the sale of specific travel and tour products.

The essential challenge for tourism suppliers and destinations is to capture and retain attention in a marketplace with a strong conceptual resemblance to a bazaar, where there are a number of major players who have developed leading brands for travel and which have already built up a large customer base. Leading travel companies are now spending very large amounts of money on building attractive and effective Web sites and developing their online brands. In these circumstances, should DMOs try to compete directly and, if so, how can they gain 'voice' in the marketplace?

If a DMO takes the view that its destination is being represented well in the Internet marketplace by commercial players, then it might reasonably question whether it should take action itself. However, many DMOs are likely to take the view that they want to gain competitive advantage for their destination and/or that commercial operators are unlikely to promote and sell the full range of products that their destination offers. For them, use of the Internet must become an integral part of their marketing strategy.

At the outset, it is important that they build up an understanding of the medium and the people who use it. The Internet is indeed a new medium, with distinct advantages over traditional media, but also, significant constraints, at least for the time being. The advantages should be exploited to the full, and the constraints acknowledged.

Where a DMO has identified target market segments in a particular market, it will be important to analyse the extent to which the Internet will provide access to those segments. Internet user surveys have been undertaken in most major markets and should provide some guidance on this.

This groundwork will enable DMOs to plan their use of the Internet with the same method and care that they would apply to their other marketing activities. Sections of this report outline current 'good practice' in Web site development and provide a step-by-step guide for DMOs to the design and development of their own sites.

Building an effective Web site is only the first stage in the use of the Internet. As explained above, it is important to be proactive in promoting the use of the Web site through traditional and electronic channels; and then, as with more conventional channels, to plan specific, carefully targeted campaigns using 'Push' marketing techniques.

DMOs start with the advantage that many consumers actively look for destination information. However, using the search engines, it is often difficult to distinguish official DMO sites from other sites (usually in large numbers) providing tourism related information on one or more destinations. There is also the problem for DMOs of how to attract the interest of consumers who may know little or nothing about their destination but have a clear idea of the type of experience they are seeking, for example trekking, bird watching, canoeing, etc.

This then leads to need for co-operation between DMOs at a strategic level to:

1. Establish portal (or gateway) sites specifically to help users search for and access official DMO Web site information. Logically, there should be a global

destination portal, linking to portals for each continent or other groupings of countries, linking in turn to national portals, and so on. These portals should provide not only the means for users to access Web sites for specific destinations, but also the facility to search to find destinations that fulfil specific requirements in terms of accessibility, attractions, events, leisure facilities, etc. and then link to their Web sites for further information.

2. Be linked from Web sites that promote specific types of experiences (sports, etc) and which may advise visitors on which countries and destinations are the most suitable for these.

3. Jointly establish partnerships with the major online travel agencies and with the major all-purpose portals to provide links to official DMO sites on a structured basis, whether directly or via destination portals as proposed in (1).

For such propositions to work effectively, it should be a requirement for the DMOs participating to ensure that their Web sites incorporate an agreed minimum range of content and that quality and integrity of the data is assured.

Measures such as these, properly resourced and skilfully executed can help to ensure that DMOs become influential players in the new marketplace of the Internet.

NEW ENTRANTS IN TRAVEL AND TOURISM INTERMEDIATION

The travel industry is going through a period of almost unprecedented change. The fast pace of development of the new consumer online technologies reviewed in Chapter 3 is causing consumers to question the added value contributed by travel intermediaries – travel agents and tour operators.

This is coming at a time when there is a growing trend towards independent travel, a trend in which tourists are showing a preference to carry out their own research into destinations and travel products, a trend which sees more travellers booking direct with travel principals. More consumers are coming to the conclusion that they do not need packagers of travel or agents to assist them. They are not only happy to make their own arrangements but enjoy doing so. Exploring the online world of travel products and destinations is fun and it is convenient. It is part of the tourism experience.

Meanwhile, for the business person who is a frequent traveller, his or her main interest is in booking a journey in the fastest, most convenient way. This could be by telephoning a travel agent, it may via the Web or it may be by using the new PC based corporate travel booking tools that are being introduced by the GDSs and some go ahead corporate travel agents. Of course, the business traveller may have a preferred airline or hotel chain and might wish to book direct. Whereas, in the past, this may have been a difficult process, the Internet has now made it viable. Travel principals are capitalising on this by providing comprehensive loyalty scheme functionality on their Web sites. The business traveller can take the opportunity to check his or her frequent flyer miles and entitlements whilst at the same time booking the next flight. In this way, the intermediary is being bypassed.

The Internet, interactive digital television and other online technologies have introduced a further threat to existing travel agents and intermediaries. They have lowered the barriers to entry for new entrants to travel. Before the Information Age, established travel agents would have taken many years to build their market presence; investing in high street retail premises with all the associated expense of shop fittings, staff, support services, computer systems, etc. The major travel agency chains worldwide have made large financial commitments through organic growth and through acquisition. Businesses such as these are not built overnight.

Contrast this with the new travel intermediaries, Internet portals like Yahoo! Travel, software companies such as Microsoft Expedia, new online agencies exemplified by Preview Travel. These are some of the new entrant online agents. They have recognised that information technology can provide them with relatively easy entry into the travel industry which is, of course, an information industry. The Internet also provides a global market for their retail businesses. Expedia, for example, which is little more than two years old has a turnover in excess of $1,000,000 per day. It sells more than 2.5 tickets every minute.

For those outside the travel industry, there is a huge opportunity to be exploited. The barriers are down and profitable entry into the industry is easier than it has ever been. For those inside, there is an urgent need to review existing models of business and develop a migration plan towards a future where e-commerce will be the preferred way to purchase travel. The new critical success factors for the travel industry are evolving and are now more favourable to new entrants.

The challenge ahead for travel companies is to understand the new game and compete with the new entrants head-on. These new critical success factors are:

- Building distribution relationships and alliances with owners of end user channels to prospective customers.

- Developing brand trust that outranks that of the competition.

- Adding more perceived value than the new entrants.

- Adopting the niche marketing strategies that are so well suited to the online era.

Travel companies must adopt a strategy that recognises these new critical success factors whilst continuing to milk the rewards of investment in existing marketing and distribution channels. There will most likely come a point in time when consumers will be at ease with purchasing travel online and travel company personnel will be located at call centre support operations rather than in high street retail premises.

New online channels have allowed a flood of new entrants into the travel and tourism marketplace. There are no longer any geographic barriers to entry and those new entrants that have built online travel retailing experience within the United States are now spreading across the world. A natural strategy for them is to enter each new market when it becomes apparent that Internet usage will soon exceed the critical mass necessary to support a profitable operation.

There is also a new type of travel industry entrant, the portal. This is an online organization that has established itself with hundreds of thousands, if not millions, of consumers as the gateway to the online world. Its own service might be a search engine or software company or a television distributor. Whichever, the important aspect is that it is used and trusted. This creates implicit brand loyalty from its consumers and so it will be trusted to sell travel.

The Internet Portals

An Internet portal is a site that users first visit when connecting to the Web. Web browser software provides a facility to set-up a "Home Page", a default Web site that will automatically be displayed when a user first goes online. It is the objective of every portal to be that default Home Page. When first signing-up with an Internet Service Provider, a consumer will be given a disk of software that, when set-up, will automatically set the Home Page to be that providers Web site. Therefore, some of the most popular portals are providers like AOL or CompuServe but portals also include search engines like Excite and HotBot and news sites like CNN. Many portals offers users the ability to customise the Home Page by deciding what type of news items should be displayed on it, so encouraging loyalty.

The portals are the controllers of distribution and every kind of travel and tourism organization, including DMOs, wishing to distribute via the Web need to consider partnering with a portal. From the portals perspective, they see travel and tourism organizations as providers of valuable content to maintain the interest of users. They are keen to partner with those that have something worthwhile to offer. Content providers interviewed by Forrester Research reported that an average of 31% of their Web site traffic was generated from their distribution partners, the portals.

According to a survey by Biznet.com, 33% of online purchasers are referred to the site where they make the purchase by a portal. The following chart illustrates which are the most popular portals.

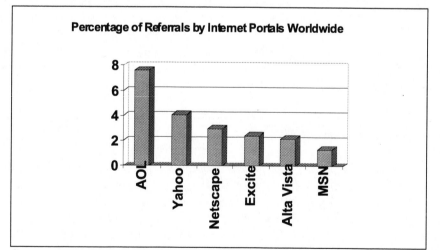

Source: Biznet.com

One could be concerned that the market will develop in such a way that there will only be a small number of portals which have sufficient traffic to warrant a distribution partnership and that just a few big players will have captured the market for online distribution. With Yahoo! now reporting 50 million page views per day, perhaps the portals will be the only way in which travel and tourism organizations can achieve widespread distribution.

The next chart illustrates that, even though the number of pages viewed at portal sites has nearly tripled, their share of Internet traffic has, in fact, not changed from October 1996 until January 1998. However, it is interesting to note Preview Travel's commitment to distributing via a portal. Preview is one of the largest travel agencies on the Web. At the end of 1997, it entered into a five year, $15 million distribution deal with the search engine, Excite.

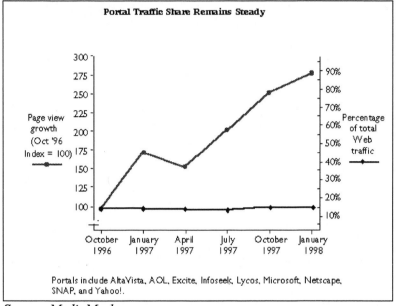

Source: MediaMark

The portals are battling for domination. If AOL maintains its domination, it is clearly ahead of its competitors. However, the stakes are high and many others such as Netscape, Microsoft and the major search engines Excite, Lycos and Infoseek will continue to fight for their share. With free Internet service provision being pioneered in Europe, AOL's business model of charging users a monthly subscription may well require reassessment. Internet penetration in Europe is on the increase. Expect this continent to be the portals' new battleground.

Case Study: Microsoft Expedia

In 1995 Bill Gate's memo 'the Internet tidal wave' marked a turning point in Microsoft's attention towards the Internet. The software powerhouse has since made significant strides in aligning its software strengths with emerging online interests. Online competencies can be broken into two core areas. Firstly, on systems side (hardware, software and networking) - including full ownership of Web TV (US) and the corresponding opportunities to use its WinCE operating system as the driving software in set-top boxes - equity stakes have been taken in the platform players eg. ntl and Telewest (UK).

Microsoft has also provided standards to bring these platforms together, based on using Windows and its associated development tools.

Secondly, Microsoft has built a series of leading online brands around its primary portal, MSN.com, including Expedia™ travel service, CarPoint™ automotive service, Hotmail, Microsoft Investor, the Gaming Zone, and Microsoft HomeAdvisor™ a real estate service.

The company had always been innovative in terms of tackling software challenges, producing products that have done well against a background of powerful marketing. Despite this success, in 1998 Microsoft appointed a new president Steve Ballmer who has since refocused the company's emphasis from the product to the consumer. With a structural reorganization in March 1999, departmental heads now enjoy a greater degree of autonomy and freedom to meet the needs of consumers.

MSN Expedia, its travel agency brand, originated from a multimedia CD ROM product concept in the mid nineties and has since evolved into one of the leading Internet travel commerce sites of the late nineties. The challenge of turning a multimedia product into one that could break down complex travel itineraries into consistent user friendly choices, a process known internally at Microsoft as Inspiration Decision Action (IDA), has been at the forefront of Redmond's 150 strong Travel Business Unit (TBU) activity. IDA is accomplished via the familiar 'wizard' walk through, eg. the hotel room wizard merges with the flight wizard giving the consumer the opportunity to reserve a hotel room at just the right time in the booking process. Microsoft Travel Technologies (MTT), the generic term for the database technologies behind Expedia, assimilate travel itineraries, eg. GDS/CRS data, into a format suitable for display on front end interfaces such as MSN Expedia, AXI TRAVEL and partner sites. AXI TRAVEL, developed with American Express, addresses the needs of corporates including managing travel buying policies, negotiated rates and expense reporting.

MSN Expedia has integrated both internally produced and licensed content. Microsoft's mapping unit has worked on making mapping technology an integral function of Expedia, eg. 'Hotel Pinpointer' has influenced hotel choice by location, while 'Driving Directions' and 'World-wide Place Finder' have also emerged on the Expedia site as useful value added functionality. MSN has recruited some of the best travel writers to provide editorial content, a fact which has been confirmed by a range of awards. Expedia content includes a comprehensive range of destination information within each section including World Guide, Expedia Magazine and From Experience.

Since October 1996, MSN Expedia has launched sites in Australia, Canada, the United Kingdom and the United States. Each product tailored to the needs of its market. Expedia UK, for example, includes 'Holiday Shop' featuring over 75,000 packages from the top 20 tour operators.

Fulfilment partners Carlson Worldchoice provides a further 200 strong telesales support team. In addition to air, car, hotel and cruise products accessible through the GDSs and Pegasus, Carlson Worldchoice provides access to 700,000 consolidated fares. Each Expedia site also benefits from a host of travel and tourism suppliers featured on the Expedia Travel Network including cruise, rail operators, tour operators and destination marketing organizations.

Consumers can link through to partners' Web sites from where they can choose to book directly either online or over the telephone. The prospect of directly connecting principals, not available through real time transaction intermediaries, is becoming a feasible option as some of the larger players add the necessary html extensions to their legacy reservation systems.

Expedia's US site alone transacts 6,000 tickets per day where weekly revenues increased from $8.5 million during early 1999 to more than $12 million by mid 1999. The Expedia Travel Network had also generated $8 million by early 1999. By mid 1999 only 2-3% of the US public had actually made travel purchases online underlining the potential in Expedia's core market.

Since its launch in October 1998 Expedia UK had sold well over $10 million worth of business by June 1999. It also has 350,000 registered users. The UK clearly underlines the potential of e-commerce within Europe. According to a recent Mori survey, 28% of UK Web users are going online each week, 32% use the Internet for travel information and to make bookings, but only 25% of respondents had actually made purchases online. 56% of respondents said they would consider purchasing flights and holidays in the future. This included 45% of respondents who would either definitely or probably buy a package holiday online.

In terms of marketing the site, MSN Expedia benefits from MSN's portal strategy which includes a channel dedicated to travel, wrapped around Expedia. MSN Expedia also co-brands as part of its Microsoft Expedia Associate programme with a number of online organizations, eg. Infoseek, Financial Times, Yell. As time goes on the true value of those partnerships will become clearer. By June 1999 all Expedia sites had a combined registered user pool of over six million.

MSN Expedia has the added advantage of being able to offer a powerful advertising medium extending across MSN sites – MSNBC, MSN.com, MSN Sidewalk and MSN MoneyCentral. Within Expedia itself, partners can also advertise in selected areas. For example, the Starwood and Hyatt hotel groups have benefited from representation in the 'Deals' section.

MSN Expedia's strategy was originally to inspire travel through first rate content. As the Internet took off online sites were generally code heavy. MSN Expedia has since come to recognise through extensive usability testing that content does not drive transactions. This is not to say MSN Expedia is withdrawing from providing top quality content but rather to utilise that content in the background and within other areas of the strategy. Increasing transactions through the site is the primary objective.

A further shift in emphasis has been to promote Expedia as a point of access to quality travel products. Expedia is not about simply allowing the customer to have total access to the cheapest products nor is it about making the industry transparent. It is about providing an electronic market place for buyers and sellers to interact. With this in mind, Expedia is going all out to meet the needs of its partners, tailoring the form of interactivity they want whether through Expedia or a co-branded site. Continually refining Microsoft Travel Technologies to respond to those needs, whilst making the customer feel more comfortable before, during and after the transaction, has been a primary objective. Responding to this objective, tactical implementations have included improving speed, accessibility, comfort and security. For instance 'RoundTrip Fare Finder' provides a one click rapid search while a credit card guarantee has helped to build trust.

DMOs can benefit from portals such as MSN Expedia which has the ability to integrate tailored transaction capabilities on-site through the Expedia Associate Programme or participation in MSN Expedia's Travel Network. During 1999 MSN Expedia worked closely with, among other DMOs, the Australian Tourism Commission. This partnership involved creating a dynamic fare board featuring the latest deals to Sydney. Expedia's value to any DMO is its ability to channel the most relevant travel options directly to the potential visitor. While funding distribution has been a low priority, due to the prohibitive costs involved, DMOs benefit from their focused presence on the Web. On the other hand, Expedia, like other portals, is keen to help DMOs implement those long sought after transaction capabilities, helping to generate inbound tourism while at the same time extending the range of travel products sold through Expedia.

By 1998 The Travel Business Unit had absorbed $100 million worth of investment over a four year period. The first fruits of the ongoing investment is the release of a totally new product in mid-1999. Combined with the launch of a major marketing campaign, the new product will be visually very different. The new code working behind the scenes, already undergoing testing, includes improved search tools, easier purchase processes, and a greatly enhanced ability for suppliers to meet their goals. Expedia's existing online presence already extends to 65% of the worlds travelling public. Expedia expects to extend its product in to Germany, Scandinavia, France and the Benelux countries.

Questions over the Euro and European harmonisation will clearly have implications on final timing, although tailoring the Expedia product to each market has been under development for some time. Europe is currently a hostile environment to do business within, with complex privacy, tax and travel regulations. Rationalisation of tax restrictions would make tax calculations easier to implement, while the removal of selling restrictions in the travel industry could increase competition and benefit the consumer. For instance, someone in France wishing to purchase a London to New York air ticket pays considerably more in France for the same ticket than they would if they could book through Expedia UK or a future release of Expedia France able to access the lowest UK fares. This issue would be true for all online travel agents operating across borders.

In summary, the key ongoing challenge for Expedia is the extent to which revenue can be derived through advertising, promotion and commission payments in the face of new industry dynamics such as the airline's continual drive towards direct selling and the lowering of commission payments. In the long term, cross border e-commerce could increase with the harmonisation of trading regulations around the world.

CHAPTER 5: DMO TECHNOLOGY CASE STUDIES

INTRODUCTION

Research has been undertaken for this report, examining how destination marketing organizations are actually embracing the Information Age. Both mainstream and smaller destinations are investing in the technology to support a new way of doing business in the Information Age.

The research work encompasses a variety of DMOs, in order that any reader will be able to find case study material relevant to his or her own organization. There is, therefore, both a geographic spread of DMOs examined, as well as a spread in size; from DMOs who have invested heavily in their Web sites and destination management systems to those who are just starting out along the road.

There are two sections within this chapter, the first looking at DMO Web sites and the second providing case studies on DMOs who have introduced integrated destination management systems. Appendix 2 provides some indicative information on the costs associated with developing DMO Web sites and destination management systems.

Destination Marketing Organization Web Sites

In order to provide an overview of the 'state-of-the-art' in DMO Web site development, twenty five sites were evaluated especially for this report and six more detailed case studies were undertaken. The twenty five were chosen on the basis that they demonstrate good practice in one or more respects. They were selected from nearly one hundred Web sites recommended by third parties, all of which were reviewed. Selection was based mainly on the attributes of the Web site, but representation was included from countries in different parts of the world and from a mixture of city, regional and national DMOs. The full list of destinations whose Web sites were reviewed is shown below.

Case Studies and Evaluated

Britain	Singapore	Spain	
West Cornwall	Zurich		

Evaluated Only

Alaska	Belize	
Edinburgh	Egypt	
Malaysia	Mexico	
Patagonia	Silkeborg	
Thailand	Vienna	

Reviewed Only			
American Samoa	Antigua	Australia	Austria
Berne	California	Cambodia	Croatia
Evian	Fiji	France	Germany
Greece	Holland	Hong Kong	Hungary
Iceland	Jamaica	Japan	Kenya
Korea	Laos	London	Luxembourg
Maastricht	Macau	Mexico	Middle East
Moscow	Namibia	New York	New Zealand
Orkney	Pakistan	Paris	Philippines
Portugal	Prague	Provence	QLD
Rio	Sarawak	South Africa	St Lucia
Sweden	Switzerland	Tunisia	Turkey
Turkey	Vanuatu	Venice	Virgin Islands
Zambia			

The following sections provide an overview of the best practice features exhibited by the 25 sites evaluated, followed by the six case studies in greater detail. Appendix 1 contains analysis tables of the characteristics and features exhibited by the 25 sites evaluated – first in aggregate, then on a site by site basis.

Overview of 25 DMO Web Sites Evaluated

Introduction to Key Features

<u>The Home Page</u>

The home page is the first point of contact most users have with a Web site. Consequently, its ability to represent a destination in a positive light and effectively communicate information is fundamental to the usability of the site and its potential for increasing consumer interest, and knowledge.

While being quite different in appearance and content, the home pages of those Web sites that were considered to demonstrate good practice had a number of things in common. Generally they all imparted a substantial amount of information, but were clearly and simply laid out. They all provided a list of the contents of the site. Many provided a brief textual description of the destination, photographs, graphics and a logo or brand.

most effective home pages were not necessarily those with the most features, those that had a range of complementary features that provided enough ion to enable a broad understanding of the contents of the entire site. Of rtance was the home page's capability of conveying a positive image of

82

The Appearance of Web Pages

The appearance of every page within a Web site is important. Looking at Web pages is a highly visual experience. Thus, while transmitting information is the goal of a Web site, it is critical that Web pages provide it in an innovative and interesting way, and without clutter or confusion.

This can be done by utilising a variety of different methods to communicate information. Substantial blocks of text can appear unexciting, be difficult to read and require more mental effort from the user than alternative forms of information transmission. The use of different colours, pictures, graphics, maps, tables and symbols break up blocks of text and substantially increase readability. The "good practice" Web sites used numerous methods to communicate information and to break up, simplify and complement text.

The use of multimedia can also be an effective way of maintaining consumer interest in a site. While forms of multimedia can take a long time to load, virtual tours and live cams are additional ways of making a site more interesting.

General Information Contained within the Site

The significance of the way information is transmitted increases if a destination has a particularly strong culture or customs, or special circumstances that should be known to prospective travellers. Additionally, information about how to get to a destination, its climate, geography, activities, events, history, telecommunications and public transport, will be very important for those individuals who do not have a base of knowledge about a destination.

Background information is often composed primarily of text. It is the kind of information that can increase clutter in a Web site. Thus the Web site should enable users to easily access the information, or skip it if they so desire. The "good practice" Web sites provided comprehensive information on a variety of subjects and had an effective indexing system which enabled users to select the information that interested them.

Interactivity - Interactive trip planners and virtual brochures

The Internet frees consumers from their traditionally passive roles as receivers of marketing communications and allows them to become active participants in the marketing process. This is a strong feature of the Internet and should be exploited. Typically the "good practice" Web sites were interactive, allowing the user to participate as much as possible in deciding which information to view and which to skip. Users are more likely to stay interested in a site's information if they have an active role in selecting that information. The best examples of interactivity were seen in those Web sites that included either interactive trip planners and/or virtual brochures.

The virtual brochure allows users to save selected pages to a clipboard, which they can save and/or later print, while the interactive trip planner generates an itinerary based on a number of criteria and specifications selected, by the user. Both require direct input from the user, thus heightening their level of involvement and potentially their satisfaction with the information generated by the site.

<u>Site Features</u>

The Internet is a form of media that requires a level of user competence not associated with any other form of media. If there are design faults in a Web site, there is a danger that a visitor may leave the site feeling frustrated. Thus a Web site should be as straightforward and easy to navigate as possible. There are a number of features that can be incorporated into a Web site that can facilitate this. Those DMO sites that were considered to demonstrate good practice included some or all of the following features to enhance their usability:

- **Link to the home page on every page.** Particularly for large sites that contain numerous pages and internal links, it is important to ensure that the user does not get lost within the site. A link to the home page on every page, will ensure that the user always has some kind of base to which they can return, if they want to view a different category of information.

- **A list of the main contents on every page.** This goes one step further than having a link to home on every page and it can save users of the site a lot of time. Rather than having to return home every time they want to view another category of information, a link at the side of the page can take them there directly. The inclusion of this feature makes navigation of the whole site simpler.

- **Search Facility.** The presence of a search facility can also save users a lot of time, by allowing them to perform a key word search of the Web site and quickly ascertain whether desired information is contained within the site. Particularly if very specific information is being sought, it can save the user a lot of time.

- **Web site available in different languages.** The Web is being used by rapidly increasing numbers of people who do not speak English as their first language. Thus the facility to read Web pages in at least three or four languages will become more and more important over time.

Special Features and Demonstrations of Good Practice

Some of the key features of the DMO Web sites will now be discussed and examples of those sites which demonstrate good practice, will be provided.

<u>The Home Page</u>

Many of the 25 Web sites had interesting and effective home pages. Amongst the best, was the home page for the NewAsia Singapore site. The home page has a black background but its main feature is a large photograph, which covers most of the area of the page. Underneath the photograph is a caption which reads "If I were in Singapore right now . . ." The photograph on the home page changes every time the site is re entered. The strength of the page lies in its ability to capture the user's attention. It is visually attractive and colourful, and also contains a clear indication of the information that can be found within the site.

The information contained within the home page of the Norwegian Web site is particularly well presented. Like many other sites, the Norwegian site has a list of internal links on the home page. However the broad categories, such as accommodation and activities appear in drop down boxes that contain subheadings, such as hostels, hotels and camping. This speeds up the process of accessing information for the user, by reducing the number of steps taken to find the information. This method of indexing is used throughout the site and is a very effective way of locating information, time effectively.

The home page of the Vienna Tourist Board also demonstrates good practice, but is quite different in appearance to any of the other Tourist Board home pages. Rather than having a textual list of the contents of the site, it has a collage of photographs that represent the different branches of the site and these may be clicked on to access the related information. Visually it is an enticing home page. It is bright and colourful and the inclusion of photographs of Vienna helps form an impression of the destination. While the home page contains virtually no text, the subject matter of the photographs clearly communicates the contents of the Web site.

The VisitBritain and Alaska home pages are quite different but are also examples of good practice. Both effectively combine the use of colour, font, graphics and photographs to capture the spirit of their destination. The VisitBritain site has many more features than the Alaska home page, yet they are both aesthetically pleasing and provide a clear overview of the contents of the site.

The Appearance of Web Pages

The Visit Cornwall site (a county region within the United Kingdom) is one of the most aesthetically pleasing Web sites. Every page is almost identical in style containing the same photograph and similar graphics and format. The site does not contain large chunks of text. It is very clearly set out and because of this is very easy to navigate and simple to use. Further description of the Enjoy Cornwall Web site can be found in the case study that follows.

General Information Contained within the Site

The Thailand Tourist Board Web site offers a large quantity of information. It demonstrates good practice by presenting the information simply and clearly. The site contains extensive information on Thailand as a whole, as well as individually on each of Thailand's seventeen regions. Information on each region is accessed via a link titled 'Province Guide' which is linked to the home page. Each of the seventeen regions has its own mini home page within the site, which contains the same directories as, and is almost identical in appearance to, the main home page. Due to the bulk of information contained within the site, there is a danger that users may become lost. However this problem is addressed by the inclusion of a direct link to the home page, the site map and the search facility on every page.

The Belize Web site and the China Web site also demonstrate good practice in the way they offer detailed information. Both sites include an excellent index system, which enables users to select only the information they desire. The presentation of both sites is simple and straightforward. They contain a lot of text but are punctuated with coloured headings, graphics and occasionally pictures, so the text is not overwhelming. The sites provide information into a wide range of subjects including government issues, history, customs, culture, events, attractions and shopping hours.

The Egyptian and Tanzanian Web sites both demonstrate innovative ways to deliver large quantities of information. They present information on a wide range of subjects including history, culture, tours and climate in the usual way. However, both also include an extensive bulletin board. Users can post questions about travelling to the destination and other users can answer the questions. Both the questions and the answers can be viewed by anyone accessing the site. This is an excellent way of communicating information on a wide range of topics that concern travellers and often addresses issues that may not have otherwise been addressed in the Web site. The Egyptian Web site also includes an online discussion forum. Users must be registered to participate. The Tanzanian Web site also has an online newsletter to which users can subscribe. It contains information concerning current affairs at the destination.

Interactivity - Trip Planners and Virtual Brochures

The Western Australian site is one of the most interactive of the 25 selected. It has an interactive trip planner, virtual brochures and an interactive database that can be used to search for information on events, attractions and destination specific information. The trip planner allows the user to request information on one or more of the following topics:

- how to get to the destination
- what to do at the destinations
- where to stay
- attractions
- events
- tours
- transport.

It then generates a list of service providers who can cater to the requirements specified by the user. The Web site gives detailed information on the service provider; including its name, address, phone and fax numbers, a photograph, pricing information and a brief description of the service offered. It also gives a direct link to the service provider's e-mail address and Web site.

The majority of the information contained within the Western Australia Web site can be saved to clipboard and later reviewed or printed to form a virtual brochure. The brochure can be edited at any time. Registration is not required to utilise the virtual brochure service.

The Western Australia Web site uses the Internet's propensity for interactivity to its full. It allows the user to define the information required narrowly or broadly and it is capable of providing a detailed, information intensive, list of results.

The Ireland Web site also has a particularly good virtual brochure service. Any information from the site can be added to the clipboard to be included in the brochure and it can be edited at any time. Registration is compulsory for first time users of the brochure service and a user name and password must be selected. These can be entered to gain access to the service on future occasions. Once registration is completed and information has been added to the virtual brochure, it remains in memory even after the site has been exited.

<u>Site Features</u>

A useful feature of the Alaska Web site is the inclusion of a photo gallery. Although there are a few pictures scattered throughout the pages of the site, the photo gallery has over thirty photographs of Alaska, which can be viewed at the user's leisure. The inclusion of a photo gallery may reduce the time taken to navigate through a Web site as pictures can substantially slow down load time.

The Zurich Tourist Board Web site was the only Web site of the 25 reviewed that incorporated an online, accommodation reservation service. The Web site has an interactive accommodation database, which can be searched, on the basis of location, type of room, price per night and price per person. The database generates a list of results and each result is rated according to how closely it matches the user's specifications. General information on the service providers is supplied along with an online reservation form. The whole process from searching the database to booking the accommodation is simple and easy. To get from the home page to submitting an online reservation, takes only four clicks.

One of the features of the California Web site that demonstrates good practice is its use of links to external sites. Due to the bulk of tourist information available on the destination, it would be difficult for one site to adequately cover every aspect. This site does not attempt to do that. Rather it acts as an excellent starting point. It offers good general background information on the destination and then a comprehensive list of links to other sites that offer more specific information on different aspects of travelling to California.

The Morocco and Hawaii Web sites are amongst those that offer users the opportunity to send virtual postcards. This is not only an effective way of drawing users back to a Web site; it is also an effective avenue through which to show photographic representation of the destination.

As a result of examining a large number of DMO Web sites - some excellent and others ineffective - the following guidelines for content are suggested:

- The home page should be information intensive, attractive and enticing. It should communicate the contents of the site and help form a positive perception of the destination.

- The pages of the site should be well maintained and information should always be current and up to date.

- Care should be taken to ensure that every page is clearly and simply set out and that information is presented in an interesting, easy to consume way.

- It should be easy for the user to ascertain what information is contained within the site and to find specific information, quickly. Relevant information not contained within the site should be linked to the site.

- Wherever possible the site should be interactive.

- Features that simplify navigation of a site and facilitate information retrieval should be utilised (Eg. An effective indexing system, a link to the home page on every page, a search facility, an email loop, photo gallery).

WEB SITE CASE STUDIES

The following case studies review in detail those Web sites considered to be of most interest.

Zurich

www.zurichtourism.ch

The home page of the Zurich Web site (a city in Switzerland) is attractive and original. As well as a list of contents, it has a collage of pictures that appear to be faded but as the cursor moves over the images they become photo quality and may be clicked on as a means of entering the site.

The Zurich Web site also has an innovative city guide section that incorporates a list of directories such as nightlife, excursions and eating out, each with a corresponding box. The user can check the boxes which correlate with their interests and hit 'go' to retrieve the available information.

The Web site also has an interactive accommodation database. The database can be searched on the basis of location, type of accommodation and price. A score is allocated to every service provider specified in the list of results according to the extent of the match between their facilities and the user's specifications. The Web site also contains a reservation system through which accommodation can be booked and paid for online.

Background

Over the past two to three years, due to a stringent financial climate and changes in the business environment, Zurich Tourism has re-structured its organization in an attempt to improve operating efficiency. Analysis of organizational operations resulted in the following goals:

- Formulation of an unambiguous mandate

- Strategic repositioning of Zurich tourism

- Performance related financing of activities and an increased marketing budget

- Boost efficiency and increase exploitation of existing potential

In August 1997, a mandate for market exploitation, product design, marketing tourist services and public relations was devised. Strategic refocusing meant targeting three well defined market segments - 'Conventions & Incentives', 'Leisure' and 'Culture & Events'.

The Zurich Tourist Board Web site was first established in 1997 as part of a university project. However the site was completely redeveloped in August of 1998. Very little external market research was undertaken in the development of the site. Internal expertise was used, as well as insight gained from trade fairs, conferences and exhibitions. Currently there is no research programme that supports the maintenance and upgrade of the site.

The site has its own budget. Funds (25,000 Swiss Francs per annum) for its development and maintenance are allocated from the marketing budget. This is just a fraction of the total marketing budget of 1.2 million Swiss Francs per year. Currently, the promotional priority of the Zurich Tourist Board is their brochures, which receive a much higher share of the budget. The Web site receives very little external funding. It contains very little banner advertising - not nearly enough to cover the costs of the Web site.

Content of the Web site is decided internally but design is outsourced to an organization called CORE Technologies. Maintenance and upgrade of the Web site is also managed internally and it is updated once or twice a week. One person is responsible for this task. The Web site has an accommodation reservation facility that is operated by an organization called Eurospider. Eurospider controls a database of accommodation service providers and a multilingual information retrieval system that supports German, French, Italian, and English. All the accommodation service providers linked to the Zurich Tourist Board Web site are members of Zurich Tourism, ensuring a degree of quality control.

Currently there are no plans for further development of or large scale investment in the Web site. The main focus for the immediate future is to upgrade the accommodation reservation system, in co-operation with other Swiss cities and the Swiss Tourist Board. For the past three years work had been undertaken to establish a national, internal, online reservation system. This is expected to be ready for release next autumn.

Zurich Tourism does not have a compulsory on line registration form but it does gather information on the way its site is used by consumers. In the months from September 1998 through to May 1999, the Zurich Tourism Web site recorded an average of 25,532 user sessions per month. Over that period, the number of user sessions grew each month to peak in May 1999 at 43,457 sessions. The following additional figures are available:

- average of 8,500 user sessions per week

- 22,000 page impressions per week

- 311,000 hits per week

- average amount of time users spend on the site = 11 minutes

Western Australia

www.westernaustralia.net

Arguably the largest state in the world, Western Australia covers one-third of the Australian continent. Western Australia has a wealth of natural resources including gold, iron ore, gas and minerals. Perth, the capital city of the State, is home to 1.38 million people.   Spanning over 2.5 million square kilometres, Western Australia is bordered largely by desert to the east, and is bound by 12,500 kilometres of pristine coastline to the west. It is famous for its blue skies, warm sunny climate and white sandy beaches. It is blessed with natural phenomena including the dolphins of Monkey Mia, the 350-million-year-old Bungle Bungle range and the towering Karri forests of the South West.

The Western Australian Tourism Commission Web site has many examples of good practice. The site represents a huge geographic area including numerous tourism intensive regions. The main strength of the site lies in the fact that it contains comprehensive information on every aspect of visiting Western Australia, yet is entertaining to peruse. Despite the large bulk of information contained within the site, it is not confusing or overwhelming. While the pages of the site frequently contain numerous internal links, every page has the main list of the site contents featured twice (once at the top and once at the bottom) making the site very easy to navigate. While the site contains a large amount of text, and is information intensive, all the pages are colourful and text is broken up by sub headings, charts, photographs and graphics making them aesthetically pleasing and substantially increasing readability.

The site is highly interactive which helps users handle the large amount of information that is available. Whether searching for information on events, attractions, activities or accommodation, the user always has the opportunity to specify from a number of categories, the specific information for which they are searching. For example, when searching for information on activities, the user can specify the region, the sub region, the activity classification from more than 100 categories and any special requirements. There is also a key word search facility.

The site also has a virtual brochure system whereby users can add pieces of information to a 'personal travel folder', which can be edited and later printed.

Background

The vision of the Western Australian Tourism Commission is to create an effective partnership between the private sector and Government and to make tourism a premier industry for Western Australia. Their mission is to accelerate the sustainable growth of the tourism industry for the long-term social and economic benefit of the state.

In 1998, the Western Australian Tourism Commission entered the third year of its five-year business plan. This was launched at the beginning of 1996 with the goal of pro-actively positioning Western Australia as a competitive force in the global tourism market. The focus in 1998 was on brand extension in response to research which showed that across all markets, Western Australia was perceived as being quiet and lacking activity. This perception was addressed by launching a comprehensive advertising campaign both domestically and in the United Kingdom, and by hosting four Olympic sport world championship events and a number of international conferences. In 1999, the focus is on converting awareness to business.

The Western Australian Tourism Commission Web site is still very young. It was launched in April of 1999. The Web site was under development for twelve months prior to its launch and extensive market research was undertaken during the design process. The content of the site was selected in-house, on the basis of research findings. The actual development of the site was completed by the Internet Centre of Excellence, which is part of a larger company, Interim Technology Solutions.

The costs of developing and maintaining the West Australian Web site is born by Western Australian Tourism Commission. A small amount of revenue is raised through banner advertising, though not nearly enough to cover costs.

Since its launch, the site has received two awards for excellence. In April 1999 it was awarded the Netscape Open Directory Cool Site Award and in May 1999 it was awarded the Best of the Web '99' Gold Award. From launch until mid-June 1999 the site had approximately 75,000 unique visitors.

Due to the newness of the Web site, the Western Australian Tourism Commission currently has no procedure in place to gather statistical information on the way in which consumers are using the site. However in due course they will adapt a software package which will enable them to capture statistics such as number of hits, user sessions and page views, monitor the most popular links, establish from which point consumers leave the site and record the average time consumers spend in the site.

Future developments for the Western Australian Tourism Commission Web site are likely to include an increase in the size of their accommodation, events and attractions database. Additionally within the next year and a half, there are plans to introduce a totally online accommodation reservation system.

Enjoy Cornwall

www.enjoy-cornwall.co.uk

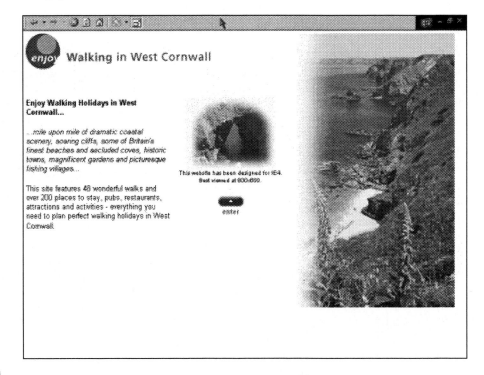

Cornwall is a county region situated in the southwest of England. The Enjoy Cornwall site is an attractive Web site, full of excellent images of the destination. This, together with the interactive nature of the site and its simple, easy-to-navigate design, are its strengths. The site presents information in an original way that is very effective. In terms of layout, almost every page of the site is identical. The only thing that changes substantially is the text, which is located in the middle of each page. At the top of each page is the table of contents for the entire site. On the right hand side of the page is a map, either of the whole area or of a specific area depending on the information being viewed. On the left hand side of the page is a list of internal links. The information content in the middle of the page can be changed by clicking on one of the specific links on the left, or by clicking on one of the general links at the top of the page, which in turn, changes the list at the left.

Another particularly useful feature of the site is the 'rucksack'. This facility enables users to isolate and gather all the information that is of particular interest to them. Users are able to add accommodation providers to their rucksack and make a booking request online. The request is followed up by the appropriate service provider.

Background

Set at the south-westerly tip of England, West Cornwall has many miles of dramatic coastal scenery, soaring cliffs, some of Britain's finest beaches and secluded coves, historic towns, magnificent gardens and picturesque fishing villages.

Walking in is one of the most rewarding ways to explore the area. Amongst the area's main attractions are its cliff-top paths and trails which allow visitors to discover the rich cultural activity which abounds across the area, from industrial heritage to tiny fishing coves. The West Cornwall Web site features 48 walks and over 200 places to stay, pubs, restaurants, attractions and activities - everything you need to plan walking holidays in West Cornwall.

Tourism in West Cornwall, is worth £217m per annum. It employs 30% of the workforce and represents 25% of the GDP. Prior to 1992, the tourism industry in West Cornwall was facing a number of difficulties. Some of these included a fragmented industry of small owner run businesses in the private sector, poor business acumen in much of the managerial staff and duplication and competition within the public sector. With the goal of combating these problems the West Cornwall LEADER project was established in July 1992. Among other things, the project led to the realisation that for promotion, print was not the only way forward.

This led to the development of the Enjoy Cornwall Web site, which was released, in early 1999. The site was part of a larger project, which also incorporated the establishment of a database of local businesses, a network of five tourist information centres and a network of forty kiosks located at key sites across West Cornwall. The public access kiosks offer customers information on various aspects of visiting Cornwall, via a touch screen interface. The kiosks promote 500 businesses and 300 public products within Cornwall.

The content and the design of the Enjoy Cornwall Web site was developed internally but design of the graphics included in the Web site was outsourced. The content of the site is updated monthly and any necessary changes to the Web site are made in-house.

Currently 3-5% of the total marketing budget is dedicated to the Enjoy Cornwall Web site. Further funding for the site comes from the 220 businesses featured on a CD-ROM and the Web site, all of whom have paid a fee for their inclusion in the site.

The following information is collected on a monthly basis:

- Total number of visitors
- Total number of page views
- Visitor numbers by day of the week
- Visitor numbers by hour of the day
- Visitor numbers by country

This information is used to inform advertisers who feature on the Enjoy Cornwall Web site and to provide insight into how the site if being used by consumers so that it can be constantly improved and updated.

Singapore

www.newasia-singapore.com:80

Virtually every aspect of the NewAsia - Singapore Web site demonstrates good practice. From the home page onwards, the site is rich in information and features yet it is clear, concise, very simple to navigate and interesting. The home page is very visual. It has a black background but is almost completely covered by photographs and graphics. It has two separate lists of internal links that also appear on every single page of the site. Therefore, whilst the site contains hundreds of pages and has many internal links, navigation is simple and it is virtually impossible to get lost within the site.

The appearance and layout of the site is one of its main strengths. Every page is visually stimulating containing a combination of text, graphics and photographs. None of the pages appear in black and white and none are composed solely of text making the pages generally more interesting and greatly increasing their readability.

The site is highly interactive enabling the user to easily select that information which is of interest and bypass the rest. It has an interactive tour planner which enables the user to enter their holiday interests and dates (up to December 2039) and receive a day-by-day itinerary. The itinerary provides the name, address, phone and fax of the service providers listed, as well as a brief textual description of the service, a photo and pricing information. Additionally, where possible it includes a direct e-mail link and a direct link to the service provider's own Web site.

The site also has a virtual brochure facility. Every page of the site can be added to a 'print cart', which can be edited and later printed.

The accommodation database is also interactive. It is possible to search the database on the basis of price, location, hotel name and key word. The information provided on accommodation providers is comprehensive including address, phone number, fax, room rates, description, facilities, a direct e-mail link and a direct link to the accommodation provider's Web site.

Background

Singapore is the major commercial and transport centre in South-East Asia. Consequently the country has a tourism industry which reflects a mixture of high yielding short-stay business and leisure traffic.

The NewAsia Singapore Web site was recently established as a replacement for the Singapore Online Guide that had previously represented the destination. The Web site is available through three/four channels and is targeted at both pre- and post-arrival markets. It is available pre-arrival through the Internet and it is available for travellers after in Singapore through a network of kiosks as well as via Singapore One, a widely available network within Singapore, which in turn is used by tourist information centres for servicing their customers.

The objective of the Web site is to deliver information on the Singapore Tourist Board activities and to project the board as an organization that is strategically driven and action orientated. It is a sophisticated multimedia tourism guide that has an image and destination positioning role as well as that of information provision.

The NewAsia Singapore Web site was developed to the specification of the marketing department of the Singapore Tourist Board.

The cost of developing, operating and maintaining the Web site is borne by the Singapore Tourist Board marketing budget. There are plans to incorporate advertisements and to achieve some cost recovery by charging for enhanced hyper-links to relevant Web sites. However, at present, no revenues are earned. The board does not expect that any eventual revenue generated will account for more that 10-20% of costs.

No figures are yet available regarding usage of the New Asia Singapore site. However, the previous, Singapore online site was registering approximately 200,000 hits per month. Additionally, HotelNet, a hotel booking service linked to the NewAsia Singapore Web site ran at about 100-200 room bookings per day.

Future developments for the Singapore Tourist Board include encouraging local tourism businesses to take electronic bookings directly from the customer rather than to go through intermediaries such as the Singapore HotelNet. Consequently there are plans to develop enhanced hyper-links via the NewAsia Singapore site to relevant tourism businesses.

Spain

http://www.tourspain.es/turespai/marcoi.htm

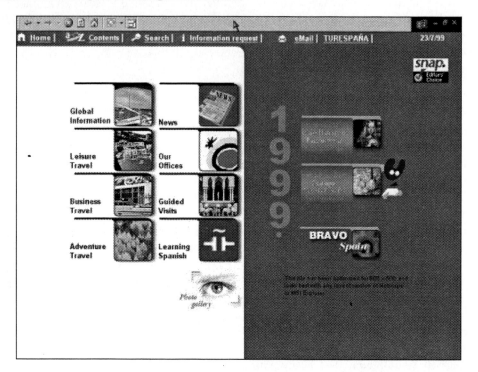

There are many examples of good practice within the TourSpain Web site. The site is very easy to navigate, with links to the home page and to the main information categories appearing on every page of the site. Also, it is easy to locate specific information within the site because there is a direct link to both a search facility and to a site map, on every page. This substantially reduces the likelihood that users will get lost within the site and increases their chances of finding required information quickly.

The site contains a wide range of information which is categorised in an effective but slightly different way to most DMO Web sites. The information within the site is divided most broadly according to the type of travel (eg. business, leisure, adventure, guided visits) while the specifics of travelling in the country (eg. regions, accommodation, transport, shopping) appear as second level headings. This allows information to be more specifically tailored to the requirements of individual travellers.

The TourSpain Web site provides a wider range of information than do most DMO Web sites. Apart from offering information on all aspects of the destination from accommodation and transport to customs, currency and shopping hours, the site provides Spanish news that has appeared in newspapers from around the world as well as links to 12 different Spanish news sources. Additionally it provides comprehensive information on Spanish language courses.

On every page of the TourSpain Web site, there is a link to an email loop and a link that enables the user to request further information. Additionally the site contains a list of all the domestic and international Spanish tourist board offices. Thus if users are unable to find some specific information or if they require additional help, they have three avenues by which they can directly contact a Spanish tourist board.

Background

The TourSpain Web site was launched on January 1 1998. The main motive behind establishing the Web site was to facilitate the cost-effective distribution of a large amount of specific, destination related information to a worldwide audience.

Market research was undertaken to develop the design and content of the site. Some of the research included studying general travel and tourism statistics. Additionally a study was conducted on the content and design of Web sites of major European national tourism offices and of major, private travel and tourism companies. This research was conducted over a period of three years, prior to the launch of the site. Approximately $150,000 were spent on the establishment of the site.

There is an ongoing research programme that supports the maintenance and upgrade of the Web site. The Spanish tourist board receives over 100 enquiries per day. Some of which are questions relating to travelling to Spain, others are suggestions for improvements to the Web site. Currently the Web site is in its third version and the enquires and suggestions generated from the Web site often act as catalysts for change in the design or layout of the site.

With market research and the suggestions from users in mind, decisions on the content of the site are left to the head of the information technology department. A Spanish company is responsible for the design of the site and has been since its inception. The company was selected after an invitation to bid for the role was published in the Official Gazette.

The Spanish Tourist Board is a government office and the Web site is funded through the national budget. However currently, in order to alleviate pressure from the state, the Spanish Tourist Board is in the process of attempting to generate revenue by calling for advertisements to appear within the site. Currently a very small proportion of the overall marketing budget for Spain is dedicated to the development of the Web site. While the site will be upgraded and improved over the next three years, its proportion of the marketing budget is not expected to be increased substantially.

The Spanish Tourist Board has solid procedures in place to gather information systematically on way its site is being used. The enquires and suggestions they receive from their Web site are used as an information source. Enquires are dealt with on a daily basis. Requests for information and suggestions are incorporated into marketing studies and the possibility of using this data for promotional purposes is being investigated.

A software package called WebTrends is used to gather various statistics on the use of the TourSpain site. These statistics are analysed and reviewed on a monthly basis. In the past twelve months the TourSpain Web site has received 100,000 unique visitors. The average amount of time each user spends perusing the site is twenty minutes.

VisitBritain

www.visitbritain.com

As well as presenting a huge amount of information in a precise and straightforward way, the VisitBritain site has a number of features that differentiate it from many other DMO Web sites. It gives consumers access to a wealth of information including access to a database with over 24,000 records which contain information on accommodation, events and activities. Searches can be run on numerous different variables, providing an effective way of locating specific information.

Another special feature of the VisitBritain site is a 'virtual brochure' which allows users to save selected pages to a clipboard, for later review, printing or saving. It is compulsory for users to register to access this facility and the feedback given provides the BTA with useful information about how the site is being used.

The site has a section specifically devoted to business travel within the UK, including a conference calendar and information on meetings, incentives and exhibitions. It is also possible to order online, the BTA's free directory, Britain The Venue, which offers a round-up of Britain's facilities for meetings, incentives and conferences. There is also a section specifically for information for the travel trade including national tourism statistics and information about excursions and trade events. The site includes extensive information for advertisers including topics such as opportunities to participate in VisitBritain, information on how to link to and from the VisitBritain Web site, as well as information on site visitors and demographics.

Background

The BTA's main functions are to promote tourism to Britain from abroad, to advise the Government and public bodies on tourism matters which affect Britain as a whole and to encourage the provision and improvement of tourist facilities and amenities in Britain. In 1997 a strategy for new media development led to over £300 000 being allocated to the development and creation of VisitBritain, the BTA Web site. Currently funding is also raised by selling enhanced entries, advertising and through securing on-site sponsorship. Funding for next years marketing activities is likely to be between £50,000 and £100,000, depending on revenue gained through sales of advertising. Working within these constraints, the BTA has extended its marketing by including the URL of the VisitBritain Web site on approximately 1 million hard copy publications distributed through their overseas offices.

During its first year VisitBritain recorded over 1 million user sessions. While they continue to steadily grow, the figures typically peak in February and April and trough between August and January. The following figures regarding usage rates are from April 1999:

- 14.2 million hits

- 1.92 million page requests

- 248 738 unique visitors

- 7.72 average requests per visit

The VisitBritain Web site has a dedicated site for each major international market as well as a global main site. These 'Gateway' sites enable the communication of specific information that may be relevant to a particular market. Gateways serve to introduce the resources of the main site and have multiple links to it.

It is not compulsory for users of the VisitBritain site to register upon entering the site. However, they must register if they wish to compile a virtual brochure. Registration gives the BTA insight into the demographic make-up of consumers accessing and using their site. 20,000 users have registered so far. The majority of registered users come from English speaking countries - the US (48%), UK (17%), Canada (7%) and Australia. All together, users of the site were located in over 90 countries.

The VisitBritain Web site has a large database of accommodation service providers, events and places to visit. This centralised database is referred to as the TRIPS database. It is compiled by nine English regional Tourist Boards and the Wales Tourist Board. Each property listed on the TRIPS database is inspected by its respective regional Tourist Board, thus maintaining VisitBritain's emphasis on quality control.

Future developments for VisitBritain are likely to include selective linkage with accommodation 'aggregators', uploading of data from the TRIPS database and a move towards vector mapping technology. This last facility allows a geographic locator to be added to each entry in the TRIPS database, so that users can zoom to street level on any online map.

DESTINATION MANAGEMENT SYSTEMS

The term 'Destination Management System' (DMS) refers to the IT and database infrastructure used by DMOs to support a broad range of their activities. A more detailed description of the different types of Destination Management Systems, their potential DMS applications and the issues that arise in implementation and operation is provided in the previous chapter in the section, "Destination Management Systems – An Overview".

The following case studies have been selected to illustrate different aspects of DMS implementation and organization in four continents by both public and private sector DMOs.

The Austrian TIScover System

Used by the Austria/Tirol Tourist Board

Overview of Key Features

TIScover 99 is a state-of-the-art DMS now used in the majority of Austrian federal provinces. First established ten years ago as an information system for the Tirol, the system has been extensively developed on a commercial basis by a wholly owned subsidiary of the Tirol Tourist Board.

TIScover 99 is a Web-based system with comprehensive functionality, including information management, distribution, reservations and electronic marketing capabilities in both English and German. It is supported by a comprehensive range of partnership agreements with leading Austrian and international organizations. These agreements include online distribution, information collection and management, technical support and industry training arrangements.

The system has now been adopted by the majority of Austria's provinces and also versions are being used in Germany and Switzerland. Industry participation, system accesses and transaction volumes are rising strongly.

Rationale

Austria has a federal constitution and the nine provinces each have their own administration. In tourism terms the Austrian National Tourist Office's main responsibility is the international marketing of Austria as a destination and it has few domestic responsibilities. Consequently the tourist boards in each province have a strong and well-established role in both domestic and cross-border marketing as well as information collection and management.

The Tirol, with over seven million visitors each year and 38 million bednights accounts for some 40% of Austria's total tourism income. The Tirolean peak season is the winter, with a substantial pre-travel information requirement, particularly by the independent short-break traveller. Accurate and timely information on accommodation availability and snow conditions is critical to travel decisions by this group.

In 1988, the Tirol Tourist Board decided to develop a comprehensive computerised tourism information system to satisfy these requirements. Much of the initial work and subsequent development was undertaken with strong academic input from Austrian universities, thus providing a coherent system approach based on sound information management principles.

During the ten years of development, the Board's overall objective has evolved to "enabling all the service providers from the entire destination to participate directly in the electronic marketplace while providing a comprehensive and accurate information service to pre- and post-arrival visitors".

History

The TIS system was first launched in 1991, initially being used only as an internal system by the Tirol Tourist Board itself. At the same time the TIS company was constituted as a wholly-owned subsidiary of the Board. In 1992 access to the TIS system was extended to about 60 local tourist offices. TIS was also an early adopter of the Internet with the first mailto:TIS@WEB site being launched in 1995.

Since 1991, there have been four new versions of the TIS system, with substantial changes or enhancements in each.

In 1997 three more Austrian provinces adopted the system and the TIS company started the process of developing partnership agreements with other parties, such as system developers. Importantly, these partnership agreements also included training and development matters and there is now a dedicated training unit in each area where TIS is operating.

Current status

The current version of the TIS system, TIScover99, is an integrated information and booking system, with different levels of functionality depending on the requirements of the destination.

The modules available to tourism operators include:

- The entry level TIScover@CLASSIC, which enables hotels or tourist boards to feed data into the system from their hotels or offices.

- At a more sophisticated level, the TIScover@PROFESSIONAL module, which allows clients to design their pages themselves and also provides for bookings via the Internet.

- The most sophisticated level, TIScover@PROFESSIONALPLUS, which facilitates the assembly of holiday packages online.

The number of accommodation facilities listed totals over 15,000 of which 4,500 are represented with detailed information and can be booked online, an increase of over 50% from the 1998 figure.

At provincial level Carinthia, Lower Austria, Upper Austria, Styria, Tirol, and Vorarlberg use TIScover99 as their only system and, through arrangements with the Austrian Hotel Association, there is national coverage of hotel accommodation.

Data Management

Local tourism organizations are responsible for the maintenance of their own data and for their local members' data to standards specified by TIScover. Individual suppliers who are directly online also have this capability. TIS maintains the overall system and management information modules. The current size of the TIScover database is approximately 4 gigabytes of data. This is equivalent to over 70,000 Web pages

Distribution

In addition to direct access via the Internet, TIScover 99 has distribution agreements for Austrian tourism products with a number of key travel-related portals. These include AOL, Expedia, TraXXX/Focus Online (the German market leader), T-Online and START Amadeus, which provides links into the GDS system.

Usage of TIScover has been growing strongly. The latest statistics available show that page views are running at over 5 million per month. Reservations and booking enquiries in the first three months of 1999 were running at over double the number in the similar quarter in 1998, exceeding 26,500 in January 1999.

Financial Aspects

TIS is funded partly from operational income and partly by the Tirol Tourist Board, but the TIS company states that it "has the scope to become self-sustainable". It receives its main income from tourism operators paying to be featured in the system and from local tourist boards and other organizations who use the system. The level of these fees is fairly modest. For example, a small accommodation provider with less than 10 rooms would pay 580 ATS (about $45) per month for the most sophisticated level of participation or 150 ATS ($12) per month for the simplest. No other fees, for example transaction dependant commissions, are charged to suppliers.

More recently, TIS has been generating significant revenues from other destinations that have adopted the TIScover system. This includes both other Austrian provinces, the German www.deutschlandreise.de and, importantly, the new KISSswiss service being established by Swiss publishers Kummerly & Frey. The City of Innsbruck has also recently adopted TIScover 99.

In principle, the company is willing to sell the system to other destinations on a comparable fee basis. However, it has adopted a policy now of only supplying DMOs and related organizations which have project management in place that fully understands the strategic and operational issues relating to DMS implementation and with the capability to establish and maintain their own services without ongoing direct involvement by TIS.

The TIS company had 17 full-time and 12 part-time employees in 1998.

Specific Strategies and Issues

TIS has a major emphasis on training and skills development so as to ensure that data maintenance, back-office functions, managing information on the Internet, designing Web sites and editing multimedia material are carried out effectively. Training courses are undertaken by a network of training 'partners' and there is a TIScover Service Centre in each of the main Austrian provinces which has as a main aim the development of centres of competence in electronic marketing.

Conclusions

The successful establishment by TIS of TIScover99 throughout Austria and in neighbouring countries reflects a number of important factors. These include the long-term support and investment of the Tirol Tourist Board, the establishment of the TIS company as an independent operating unit, the strong historical emphasis on information science, the provision of services tailored to TIS' main customers in the tourism industry and the development of effective partner relationships with a wide range of public and private sector complementary organizations.

The Finnish Tourist Board Systems: MIS, PROMIS and RELIS

Overview of Key Features

The Finnish Tourist Board (FTB) has developed and operated an integrated suite of tourism-related networked services for use by the Finnish tourism organizations and industry. These include:

- MIS, the Board's own Market Information System

- PROMIS, the Professional Marketing Information Service, a tourism database covering the whole of Finland

- RELIS, the Research, Library and Information Service.

Substantial elements of all of these databases are also now accessible via the Internet through FTB's Online Travel Guide.

The current applications focus primarily on information management and delivery to and from a range of users including the Finnish tourism industry as well as domestic and international tourists. Transactions are not handled directly by the Finnish Tourist Board but there are direct links from the Online Travel Guide to the reservation services of individual companies or municipalities, as appropriate.

A range of country-specific pages within the Online Travel Guide have been or are being developed for key markets such as Germany, France, the Netherlands, Russia and USA. These act as local language 'gateways' to the Online Travel Guide and additionally have specific information on relevant products available in each market such as tours and transportation.

Rationale

Finland is a relatively small and "off the beaten track" destination. The strategy of the Finnish Tourist Board is to work together with the Finnish tourist industry and other interest groups who share common goals so as to maximise the country's reach and impact in the international marketplace. Information technology is regarded as a powerful tool for this – not just to provide an electronic presence at the point of sale but also to foster collaboration between the different industry sectors.

An early goal was to improve the cost-effectiveness of the Board's work by simplifying and speeding up work processes, reducing duplication of activity and improving FTB internal and external communications. The successful implementation of the Board's IT initiatives has also provided an effective technical environment for the Finnish travel industry to develop applications for their own use.

Specific emphasis is made in Finland's overall tourism strategy to "the clear profiling of the nation's tourist image, the precise segmentation of customers and markets and the effective marketing and distribution of products". It is not surprising that a country that has probably the highest levels Internet and mobile phone usage in the developed world should have adopted IT so intensively as a tool to achieve this aim. The Market Information System (MIS) in particular enables the FTB and their trade partners to manage and organise sales and marketing campaigns world-wide.

History

MIS was launched in 1992, initially as an internal system for FTB but access was soon extended to professional users within Finland. Lotus Notes was used as the basis for the system and an updated version was introduced in 1997.

The PROMIS product database was launched in 1995 and by 1998 was already on version 4, reflecting the speed of technological development and changes in user requirements.

The RELIS system became operational in February 1997. All PROMIS information providers have access to the RELIS system and vice versa. Parts of RELIS are also available via the Internet in the Tourism Dataline section of the Online Travel Guide.

Current Status

The Market Information System (MIS) is a data management and distribution system which is used and maintained by all staff within the Finnish Tourist Board. It is also used by FTB to manage and organise specific sales and marketing campaigns. It has eleven core MIS applications covering the whole range of tourist board and travel industry activity. For example:

- the Buyers & Media application contains tour operator and travel agency profiles together with contact information. It also holds basic data on major media in key markets.

- the RMS Marketing Plan applications holds details on all marketing plans, promotional campaigns and their related actions from all Finnish Tourist Board offices world-wide.

- the extremely popular Mekkala application functions as an electronic notice board for the whole of FTB world-wide, providing an efficient platform for internal discussions and news, the posting of proposed presentations and other internal corporate communications.

Other MIS applications include information on European Union initiatives and decisions that relate to the Finnish travel industry, statistical data, general information about Finnish Tourist Board's offices and personnel as well as data on FTB working groups, projects and their status reports. There is a specific Contact application to manage seminar and workshop documentation and correspondence as well as FTB customer contact information and a Webdocs application, used to create bespoke Internet sites for different country or market requirements.

The Professional Marketing Information Service (PROMIS) is the national database of Finnish travel products and services. It provides all PROMIS, RELIS and MIS users with a wide selection of up-to-date information on travel products, services and contact information. The data are maintained by different parties. For example general Information on Finland as a destination is maintained by FTB. External PROMIS partners such as regional and city tourism organizations maintain data on tourism services, events, attractions and their own towns, cities or regions. Currently the database holds tourist information from 422 Finnish municipalities and counties though the quality and depth of information can vary.

Updates to the PROMIS database by information providers are automatically converted into HTML and transferred to the common Internet server daily and from there to the relevant section in the Online Travel Guide as well as being available to all MIS, PROMIS and RELIS users.

Importantly, certain PROMIS information is copyright free and can be downloaded by PROMIS partners for use in brochures and other marketing publications. Similarly the partners are able to use the data in their own IT applications, such as Web sites and CD-ROMs.

The Research, Education and Library Information Service (RELIS) was developed for use in national travel research, product development, education and libraries. All PROMIS partners have access to the RELIS system and vice versa. Thus RELIS provides an up-to-date, easy to use information system that connects the travel industry to research and education organizations. Parts of RELIS are also available on the Internet through the FTB Web site in the Tourism Dataline section.

FTB's Web site, the Online Travel Guide, draws on these three applications. Currently the Web applications are text only so as to optimise browsing and printing speeds, though clearly there is the capacity for presenting multimedia data as well and certain extranet applications are currently under development for professional use.

Financial Aspects

The core MIS, PROMIS and RELIS systems are funded by FTB and operate on a non-commercial basis. The majority of data within PROMIS is collected and maintained by tourism offices in Finnish regions and municipalities who pay approximately 250 euros per month for user and support services for each PROMIS server. Total set-up costs are not available but are cited as being "surprisingly modest". The whole operation was managed essentially by one executive until 1997.

Related Systems

FTB also has two commercial subsidiaries which undertake related work. One, Comma Finland Oy, is owned 49% by FTB and undertakes a range of print production and similar work for FTB and the Finnish travel industry. Its photographic archive has recently been made available to publishers worldwide as a digital photobank.

The second, NordInfo GmbH, is a marketing services company and is 100% owned by FTB. In turn NordInfo owns 100% of Finnova Skandinavia AB which provides customer service for consumers, travel agencies and tour operators, distributes brochures, and arranges exhibitions, fairs and campaigns. Finnova now also operates the Helsinki Hotspot information and ticket office which opened in Stockholm in 1997.

Together these three companies now employ over 30 staff and represent a significant area of commercially-focused activity for FTB, supplementing its core information activity.

FTB has been charged by the Finnish Government with increasing the extent private sector contributions to its budget and some changes to the existing arrangements can be expected in due course.

Conclusions

The Finnish Tourist Board has in many ways pioneered the use of IT as an integral part of a National Tourist Office's operations. The Board believes that IT has been an effective tool for developing cross-industry co-operation within Finland, as well as for reaching a world-wide audience. FTB has demonstrated that, through effective management of the various projects, the use of industry standard software, the direct relationship and response of the projects to user requirements, it is possible to develop significant systems without massive financial investment. Total staff numbers at the Helsinki office of the Board have also been considerably reduced during the period of implementation from over 90 to just over 50.

The Irish Gulliver System

Used by the Irish Tourist Board and Northern Ireland Tourist Board

Overview of Key Features

Gulliver was first established in 1990 as a joint venture between the Irish Tourist Board (ITB) and the Northern Ireland Tourist Board (NITB). It is one of the earliest examples of a comprehensive DMS.

Gulliver is now operated commercially. A private Irish financial services company is the main shareholder, but the Irish and Northern Ireland Tourist Boards together retain a 26% shareholding. Also, the data held within Gulliver continues to be owned by ITB and NITB.

In addition to being a database for the entire range of Irish tourism products, Gulliver is used to support the growing activity of the main shareholder's dedicated call-centre. This centre provides both advance travel information and reservations to its customers, mainly via toll-free lines.

Gulliver has several other applications, including its use by tourist information centres (TICs) throughout Ireland, as the data source for public access kiosks and, since 1998, as a branded element within the Irish Tourist Board's Web site.

Rationale

The market for tourism to both parts of Ireland has been heavily influenced by political factors for many years. Historically it has also been substantially dependent on ethnic and VFR (visiting friends and relatives) traffic with a short peak season in the summer that led to capacity problems. This pattern is now changing and Dublin in particular has become established as a major year-round European short-break destination.

The industry is characterised by a large number of small-scale accommodation providers, the majority of which belong to co-operative marketing groups of one kind or another.

At its inception in 1990, Gulliver's primary objective was to become "the main channel of distribution for information and reservations on all major aspects of tourism in Ireland". A major priority was to develop a comprehensive destination information system with online reservation services for the full range of accommodation products in Ireland, in order both to reduce peak season capacity problems and to support marketing activity.

Substantial European Commission funding has been available under various programmes. Cross-border activities between the Republic of Ireland and the United Kingdom in particular were eligible for support.

History

Gulliver was launched in 1992. In its early stages it experienced both technical and operational problems. Specific problems included the high costs of centralised real-time computing and the leased lines used for communications. Initial plans to set up direct links with key airline CRSs were not realised and the volume and value of transactions being handled by the system failed to meet expectations.

The move to a commercial operation was prompted by a major strategic review of Irish tourism undertaken in 1997, as well as by official criticism of the high costs incurred since the inception of the projec. The successful privatisation of the company in 1997 was a major step forward, though it has inevitably introduced new issues of balance between private and public sector operations.

Current status

Gulliver has two basic and inter-related functions. It operates as a national database of Irish tourism products, holding, for example, data on all the hotels and other accommodation providers in Ireland that are classified under the Irish Tourist Board's voluntary but comprehensive accommodation classification scheme. This data forms the core of the Gulliver Web site, one of the most advanced of its kind in the world.

Secondly Gulliver operates as a commercial service handling information enquiries and reservation requests, both over the counter at TICs (run by Ireland's Regional Tourism Organizations) and through the Gulliver Call Centre located in the far West of Ireland at the main shareholders head office. This service is available seven days a week and is on a freephone basis from most, though not all, markets.

Call levels during the summer of 1998 were running at approximately 2,000 per week, being handled by a team of 70 agents. It is estimated that approximately 25% of inbound calls to its call centre are converted to a reservation.

Financial Aspects

Properties in the Gulliver database pay an annual fee depending on type of property and size of between 6.50 and 50 euros. 10% commission is then payable either to the main private shareholder/system operator (for bookings via the call-centre) or to Tourist Information Offices (for bookings made through them). Additionally a small flat fee per booking is charged to the call-centre's customers. Accommodation availability is held on either an allocation or on a request basis. Only allocated rooms are available for automated bookings.

The majority private owner and system operator now has the main responsibility for defining new functionality and for general business development issues. For example, it has set up user groups through organizations such as the Irish Hotel Federation, so as to ensure that development plans meet the requirements of the accommodation industry.

Specific Strategies/Issues

While from an NTO perspective, the rationale for Gulliver remains substantially the same as originally envisaged (ie. the effective electronic presentation of the Irish tourism product in the world marketplace), the move to a commercially operated service has obviously changed the parameters within which decisions are taken.

A key issue has arisen regarding the role of Gulliver in relation to the traditional activities of US travel agents and tour operators. The US market is of great importance to Irish tourism and there are numerous tour operators and agencies there that specialise in tours to Ireland. Clearly a Web site on its own has the potential to help individual customers deal direct with suppliers, facilitated, naturally in the case of intending US visitors to Ireland, by the lack of language barriers and the widespread use of the Internet in the USA.

This threat of 'disintermediation' has been much debated in the United States, where there is an extensive travel agency and specialist tour operator community. Substantial proportions of agency business are accounted for by leisure traffic and agency revenues are under extreme pressure because of the commission capping policies of the majority of airlines.

Consequently concerns quickly arose over the arrangements reached between the two tourism boards and their private sector partner, which appeared to give the operator a privileged position in regard to handling bookings. Discussions were held during 1998 with US operators but no resolution was achieved and, in January 1999, a leading US specialist tour operator to Ireland, Brendan Tours, filed suit in Dublin alleging that the Irish Tourist Board was seeking to create a monopoly. The action was supported by a considerable number of other US and European tour operators as well as the American Society of Travel Agents (ASTA) and the US Tour Operators Association (USTOA).

At the time of writing it is understood that negotiations were taking place between the parties. Clearly it is in every party's interest to avoid a lengthy legal struggle and to reach a settlement which addresses the legitimate concerns of affected parties.

Conclusions

Gulliver has travelled along a long road since its inception nine years ago and heavy expenditure has been incurred. It is only since its privatisation and the implementation of the Gulliver Web site and call centre that it has become a significant force in international marketing terms. However this has also led to a degree of conflict with established distribution channels, as noted above. The precise outlook for Gulliver remains unclear, not least because of the potential impact on turnover and financial results of new arrangements needed to resolve the current conflict with established players.

Namibia Wildlife Resorts Central Reservation System

Used by Namibia Wildlife Resorts

Namibia, a member of WTO since 1997, is an emerging tourism destination in Southern Africa. A substantial proportion of the country's key tourism resources are represented by the assets of the Namibia Wildlife Resorts (NWR) company. Previously these 24 resorts, comprising huge areas of national park and their associated infrastructure, were state-owned and operated as the "Government Resorts".

The Namibian Government sets a high priority on sustainable development and efficient inventory management of the NWR product offer is vital to the success of this policy. A central reservation system was first introduced by Government Resorts in 1993. This system is now outdated and both it and its associated business processes are being reviewed and upgraded to meet the present and future requirements of NWR, its customers and the Namibian Government.

The new NWR system is intended to be a fully functional reservation system for Namibia's key tourism assets, bringing the concept of "Destination Management" fully into operation. As planned, the new NWR system could also represent an important move towards the development of a larger DMS, serving the rest of the Namibian tourism industry.

Rationale

Tourism is considered by the Namibian Government to have a major role in the future economic development of the country. A new tourism policy is being introduced based on sustainable development principles. This policy has been developed in conjunction with a long term assistance programme, the Namibia Tourist Development Programme, (NTDP) of the European Union under the Lomé Convention.

The country's primary tourism product consists of wildlife and culture within the natural environment. This high quality but very fragile resource base makes it imperative to control carefully the tourism development process. The focus is not however restricted purely to high yielding tourism, as there is also an emphasis on Community Based Tourism Enterprise development with the objective of involving local communities actively in the tourism sector.

The importance of adopting sustainable development policies is reflected by the fact that Wildlife, Conservation and Tourism responsibilities have been grouped in one Ministry since 1990. This is now the Ministry of Environment and Tourism (MET). The effective control of tourism numbers at specific locations is an important goal for MET and since the NWR assets represent such a high proportion of the country's total accommodation stock, especially in sensitive locations, they are central to this overall policy.

The NTDP and a Government White Paper established the overall objectives for the industry. As part of this process the parastatal Namibia Wildlife Resorts is in the process of being established. Its main assets are the twenty four resorts and their associated accommodation facilities previously known as the Government Resorts. Access control, effective inventory management and distribution by NWR will be central to its future success. An efficient central reservations service with links to both the resort facilities themselves and to international distribution networks is therefore required.

History

In 1993 the reservations system for the Government Resorts was computerised centrally in Windhoek. Reservations were accepted by mail, in person and over the telephone via the central switchboard. Email facilities have been recently introduced. In theory there was on-line communications to the resorts but, in practice, availability had still to be checked by telephone.

The hardware and software has been continuously upgraded to meet specific and changing requirements, but numerous technical and business process issues have considerably reduced the intended efficiency of operation.

For example, all payments for pre-booked accommodation have to be made in person at the central office and as many as one third of all customers arrive without knowing whether they actually have a confirmed reservation. Similarly local or international tour operators, who play an important role in sourcing and producing business for the resorts, have no automated access to the system. Also, although tour operators have been able to block book accommodation they have received no commission or discounted rates and consequently have had to charge higher rates than those available to customer booking directly with the centre.

Consequently a detailed review of both hardware and software needs was undertaken in 1997. This study took into account not only the apparent under-performance of the existing system but also the potentially different operating policies which were likely to be adopted by the management of the new NWR.

Current Status

NWR was formally established on April 1, 1999, and staff recruitment is in progress. Equipment and systems used in the reservations and call centre of the Government Resorts have been transferred to NWR.

A Work Programme under the NTDP was approved in May 1999 and is underway. The specification and procurement of the new Reservations System is one of the major components of this programme.

Specific issues that are being addressed include the need to have full real-time inventory control and online links to the individual resorts, connection to the Internet and commercial networks such as the GDSs, an integrated accounting and billing system and improvements to the operating procedures within the central reservation office. As this functionality is added, the system will start to move from a purely reservations system to take on the characteristics of a DMS.

Financial

The total capacity of the NWR is substantial. It has around 1600 beds and an equivalent number of camp site places, thus representing the majority of leisure-related accommodation in the country. Current occupancy rates are around 50%, so NWR assets account for the majority of non-business overnights in the country. Accurate financial statistics as to turnover and profitability are not currently available as they were not kept by the Government Resorts organization

Full details of the financial plans for the new system are not yet available, as the NWR company is not yet fully staffed and operational. However, as the system will be operating as an integral and central part of the whole NWR operation, rather than as a stand alone DMS, the business case will be similar to that of a normal resort or tour operator, and not have to take account of the more complex factors invol;ved in many other DMSs. Thus all reservations for NWR will be processed by it, whereas a more typical DMS processes only a small fraction of a destination's capacity.

Specific Strategies and Issues

The current plans for the redevelopment of the NWR system include a substantial focus on business planning and staff training. Making a successful transition from a publicly run resorts operation to a commercially operated company is not an easy process, but will be critical to the new company's success.

Future service levels of the new company will be dependent not just on the successful specification and procurement of the new system but also on the staff who operate the service and the processes it is required to support.

Conclusions

The establishment of NWR is being carried out as part of an integrated restructuring and redevelopment programme for the whole of Namibian tourism. Within this, the role of the NWR central reservation service is correctly regarded as being central not just to the new company's commercial performance, but also to the contribution which the company can make to the Namibian government's overall policy of developing sustainable tourism policies.

The importance of NWR's position as the operator of the country's key tourism and accommodation resources cannot be overstated. DMSs in other countries neither control their own inventory nor effect the majority of accommodation reservations. Consequently the new NWR system will in effect be one of the most comprehensive actual DMSs in operation anywhere in the world, as well as being able to provide a facility for the whole of the Namibian tourism industry.

The assistance provided to date via the Namibian Tourism Development Programme has been and continues to be vital in supporting the process of restructuring the operational core of the largest part of the country's tourism resources.

Canadian Travel Exchange (CTX)

Used by the Canadian Tourism Commission (CTC)

Overview of Key Features

The Canadian Tourism Commission launched the Canadian Tourism Exchange, known as CTX, in May 1999. Claimed to be a "first of its kind" anywhere in the world, CTX had already been operating a pilot of this Internet-based interactive industry-wide communications system for the tourism industry for just over a year.

CTX is essentially an Extranet operating as a national communications and knowledge transfer tool for Canadian tourism industry members. Its over-riding objective is to improve the competitiveness of the Canadian tourism industry. Thus CTX is not a traditional Destination Management System targeted at consumers. However it does contain a searchable database of those product suppliers and purchasers who are members, so that, for example, a European tour operator who is a CTX member can search for specific products within CTX.

Membership of CTX is free but access is password based. It is bilingual (English/French) and open to members of the Canadian tourism industry and those with interests in Canadian tourism elsewhere in the world.

Key features currently operating include access to comprehensive reports and statistical data on tourism related subjects, discussion forums, the ability to manage contact groups, advertising and promotion opportunities, a news service which can be specified and filtered according to the interests of the individual member and a series of inter-linked Web sites.

Rationale

Canada is a large and sparsely populated country. It has a federal constitution and has ten provinces and three territories. The Canadian Tourism Commission, established in 1996, embodies the Federal Government's responsibilities for Canadian tourism, with a requirement from the Federal Government to operate and be financed on a public/private partnership basis. In 1998, CTC had a budget appropriation from the federal government of US$66 million and a significantly larger contribution from the tourism industry of US$83 million. The CTC is currently being reconstituted as a Crown Corporation in order to orientate it more closely to the private sector and to provide it with greater managerial and financial freedom. Each province and territory has its own tourism body on a public/private sector partnership basis and the majority has long been operating some form of DMS, usually including a call-centre. Notable examples include the Check In service in Nova Scotia, first established in 1986, and the TraveLinx operation in Ontario, developed and managed by a major telephone company on behalf of the Ontario government.

The existence of these established operations and the earlier experience with BOSS-Tourism (see below) means that there is little or no rationale for the development of a federal DMS in the traditional sense. However the size of the country and the fragmented nature of the Canadian tourism industry creates a real need for effective communication between the different players. Like the US, Canada has high levels of Internet usage and therefore the concept of an Internet-based industry extranet was developed in order to mobilise the efforts of the industry under the leadership of the CTC.

History

CTC's predecessor, Tourism Canada, had developed a tourism section within the Federal government's Business Opportunities Sourcing System (BOSS). BOSS was originally a mainframe hosted online database developed in the early 1980's to hold data on Canadian businesses, especially in manufacturing.

BOSS-Tourism was first established in 1991 as a database of "export-ready" tourism products. Again, entry into the database (membership) was free and, by 1992, some 3,200 Canadian tourism businesses were registered. The need to use a modem and dial-up to connect to its system inhibited widespread use of BOSS-tourism and a one year pilot in 1994 with World Travel File, a product database linked to Sabre, was not extended.

The CTC took a policy decision in 1996 to focus on the development of "better communications for the Canadian tourism industry" and the CTX pilot was initiated in mid-1997.

Current Status

CTX is now operational, but some sections are not yet open for use. In June 1999 there were nearly 4,000 CTX members and it contained data on over 9,000 organizations. These numbers are forecast to nearly double by the end of 2000.

There are four sections (or Exchanges) to CTX - Information Exchange, Promotions & Marketing Exchange, Employment Exchange and Meetings Exchange. Of these, only the Information Exchange is fully operational, though the Promotions and Marketing Exchange is partially open.

Within the Information Exchange there is a focus on industry communication, both by CTC to the Canadian tourism industry and between its members. The Tourism News section, for example, not only contains tourism and travel industry news items posted by industry publishers, Baxter Publishing, but also has the facility to accept news items posted by any member.

Members can specify (and change) their news "preferences" at any time in an easy to use method and items can be saved in a series of personal folders. Push technology is also employed so that members can receive notification of new items that correspond to their specified preferences. There is also a search function that covers both current and archived information.

There are some twenty Discussion Forums currently available on topics such as Relationship Marketing and Ecotourism, the majority of which are accessible to any CTX member, though some are restricted to specific sub-groups of the membership.

Members can also easily set up specific contact groups within CTX, enabling them for example to mail promotional offers to selected partner organizations. Additionally, links to individual members' corporate Web sites are incorporated when requested and there are powerful search facilities enabling users to identify potential partners or suppliers.

CTX is also linked directly to the Canada Specialist programme operated by CTC. This is a training and membership group open to travel agencies and other organizations who specialise in selling Canadian tourism products. The direct link between the Canada Specialist Web site and CTX provides rapid but privileged access by users to a far wider range of product and contact information that previously possible.

Financial Aspects

Membership of CTX is free of charge. Start-up costs were fully funded by CTC and are estimated to have been over US$3 million up to the launch in May this year. The budget for the current year is US$2 million for technical services and US$450,000 for marketing.

Costs are expected to rise as functionality increases, membership grows and system usage expands. Estimated development costs for the next two years are US$2 million.

Specific Strategies and Issues

The extent to which CTX develops will depend on a mix of inter-dependent factors including the extent to which it can provide added value to its members and the extent to which the same members participate, contribute and exploit the opportunities open to them.

Current efforts are focused on establishing full functionality and optimising the use of CTX, rather than on developing associated commercial services, but clearly there is an opportunity for this to be done, probably in partnership with other parties.

Conclusions

CTC has taken a radical but focused approach to addressing the issues of cross-industry communication and competitiveness through the development of CTX. It clearly complements rather than competes with existing DMS services provided at provincial level. CTX also has major potential for the future development of international marketing and for partnership arrangements within the Canadian tourism industry.

South Pacific Islands Travel Channel

Used by The Tourism Council of the South Pacific (TCSP)

Overview of Key Features

The Tourism Council of the South Pacific (TCSP) is a grouping of thirteen destinations in the region which are co-operating in a long term tourism development programme supported by European Union funding.

A central TCSP database has been in existence for some years, co-ordinated by TCSP headquarters in Suva, Fiji. In 1996, a hosted Web site serving the TCSP countries, SPICE, was developed and maintained using information from this database.

SPICE has now been amalgamated with the South Pacific Islands Travel Channel, one of a developing group of Travel Channels in Australasia operated by Jasons Publishing Co. of New Zealand.

Rationale

The TCSP comprises the following thirteen island nations - American Samoa, Cook Islands, Fiji, Kiribati, New Caledonia, Niue, Papua New Guinea, Samoa, Solomon Islands, Tahiti, Tonga, Tuvalu and Vanuatu. The remote and dispersed nature of the islands (Fiji alone has over 300), spread across a vast region of the South Pacific and with a fragmented and small-scale tourism offer, means that although there is a strong South Pacific "image" the destinations themselves have little individual recognition.

Thus there is a strong argument for regional co-operation in marketing as well as the development of environmentally sustainable tourism. The latter is particularly important in view of the special characteristics of the region's ecology.

The majority of tourism traffic to and within the region is international. It is either handled by specialist agencies or arranged individually. There is therefore a major requirement from individuals for pre-travel information regarding the entire region.

History

The TCSP was established as a vehicle for tourism co-operation in the early 1990s, with financial support from the European Union. A feasibility study into the potential for a regional DMS, incorporating both information and reservation facilities, was undertaken in 1992, but technical and commercial factors militated against the establishment of a reservations service.

However a central database of TCSP members' product information was established at TCSP headquarters in Suva, Fiji, and, with the advent of the Internet, a decision was taken to develop a TCSP Web site, SPICE. This site was established in 1996. Updates from the Suva database were automatically fed into the SPICE site, but it became apparent that there was scope to enhance the usefulness of the site and a link-up with a specialised publisher was proposed.

An arrangement with Jason Publishing of New Zealand, which also operates the new Zealand and Australia Travel Channels, was reached in 1998 and the new South Pacific Islands Travel Channel was launched in October last year.

Current Status

The South Pacific Islands Travel Channel now combines information, pictures, maps and sound files from the existing libraries of Jason Publishing Co Ltd and other partner travel publishers including the TCSP. It also contains direct links to member countries' own Web sites where appropriate.

Jason Publishing describes the site as "an aggregated content Internet site". In essence, this is a publishing version of a department store or shopping centre which houses many different retailers. Providing a regional Internet portal for the Web pages of a number of travel and tourism content partners makes it easier for Internet users to find and access the sites than via a variety of different "entrances".

For the TCSP and its members, the main benefits of participating in the South Pacific Islands Channel are cited as being "the ability to obtain a high quality, powerful and effective Web site solution at a fraction of the real cost and time involved in establishing and maintaining a stand-alone Web site with similar accessibility and performance standards". In other words in developing a regional Web site it can be more cost-effective to work in partnership with others who have similar objectives, than to try to do everything on a stand-alone basis.

Other related benefits include enhanced regional co-operation with the various private sector partners involved and the benefits of co-operative marketing of the site and its services through cross-promotion in traditional printed media.

No central reservation facilities are yet offered by the South Pacific Islands Travel Channel, but direct links to individual partners' Web sites for bookings and booking requests are offered when feasible. All operators have an enquiry form attached to their Web pages which can be used to take reservations. For security purposes, Secure Socket Layer (SSL) Encryption Technology and a Verisign Authentication Certificate are used. This means that information sent by a user is encrypted during transmission and, importantly, the system verifies that the actual server being used by the customer is the real server operated by Jason Publishing and not a copy set up for fraudulent purposes by others.

Financial

The South Pacific Islands site has been developed by Jason at no cost to TCSP. Revenue is generated through advertising. Additionally TCSP members who wish to have an enhanced entry receive a discount on normal tariffs. The agreement with TCSP requires that the South Pacific Islands Travel Channel should be comprehensive. Consequently the total number of operators featured in the site is greater than the total TCSP membership. Much of this data has been sourced from Jason's existing regional database.

Strategies/issues

Jason Publishing states that the current content represents only the first stage in its expansion of the South Pacific Travel Islands Channel site, an entirely natural commercial ambition. The extent to which such expansion can remain synergistic with the requirements of the TCSP for destination promotion is not yet known, but is likely to be high since both parties are interdependent and both will gain from the success of the current relationship.

As long standing regional publishers, Jason do not see themselves as travel agents and do not have a strategy to take commission income from the site. Rather they seek to route enquiries and reservations direct to featured operators or businesses and to leverage their existing print publications through the Internet and vice versa.

Conclusions

The TCSP as a partnership has taken a logical step in fostering a further partnership with an established commercial publisher with a strong regional presence. Success will depend on the extent to which the South Pacific Islands Travel Channel can provide added value to all parties, including the tour operators featured on the site.

The facility for direct links to individual operators and establishments from a verified site will be important for the growth of transaction volumes and, in conjunction with an effective search facility, it may obviate any need for a traditional type of DMS reservation facility operated by TCSP or a partner company.

CHAPTER 6: STEPPING INTO THE INFORMATION AGE

INTRODUCTION

There is every reason why destination marketing organizations should be participating on the Web and no excuse to not do so. Whilst some DMOs are spending millions of dollars in implementing sophisticated integrated systems, it is perfectly possible to develop a Web site that may require an initial investment of just thousands of dollars.

In this chapter, we provide destination marketing organizations with guidance on how to participate in this new online world. Advice is given on how a DMO should tackle the task of developing a presence on the Web. An outline guide to developing a destination management system is also provided.

A further section in this chapter looks at how tourists will purchase travel in the Information Age. How will they shop and what are the implications for travel and tourism organizations? There is a major role here for smart cards and their potential as financial instruments and unique identifiers is examined.

DEVELOPING A PRESENCE ON THE WEB

For the reasons outlined previously, most DMOs should be developing their use of the Internet, initially through implementation of a well-designed Web site. DMO Web sites vary from the sophisticated, forming an integral element of a Destination Management System, to simple stand-alone sites. Whatever their level of sophistication, some work well, and some do not.

This section offers a step-by-step guide to help you to develop a Web site that will meet your customers' expectations. You may not be able to achieve everything at once, and you should plan on a major upgrade to your site at least in the medium term.

The Role of the Internet within the Overall Marketing Strategy

The first step is to consider the role of the Internet within your overall marketing strategy. Start by setting your objectives, which may include one or more of the following:

(a) To increase business for your destination and your tourism suppliers

(b) To generate revenue for the DMO

(c) To improve communications and relationships with more targeted groups

(d) To reduce costs

(e) To create good PR for your destination and/or your organization.

The Internet can provide a cost-effective tool for meeting any of these objectives, but you may wish to concentrate on one or two of them initially and build in others in a later phase.

The ways in which the Internet can help you achieve these objectives, providing the functionality of the site is carefully specified and the design is well thought out, are as follows:

(a) To increase business for your destination and your suppliers, by

- raising awareness of your destination and the type of emotional experiences it offers

- providing information about things to do and places to stay

- enabling customers to easily and securely book both accommodation and other relevant tourism products that are required for the trip

- offering last minute deals and special offers, targeted to consumers with a high propensity to buy.

(b) To generate revenue for your DMO, by:

- taking commission on sales and charging fees to tourism service providers

- selling products and services on line, such as travel insurance, local produce etc

- selling advertising and generating third party sponsorship.

(c) To improve communications and relationships:

- with customers, through feedback forms, chat rooms and newsgroups

- with tourism product suppliers, through online services like market intelligence, forums for news and debate, updating of availability information.

(d) To reduce costs by:

- directing enquiries to the Web site rather than by sending a printed brochure

- allowing suppliers to maintain their own data online

- targeting potential customers more efficiently through relationship marketing and analysis of data on the use of the site.

(e) To create good PR by providing:

- links to other useful sites and organizations

- corporate information on the site

- up-to-date news and press releases online.

In most destinations, it will be a high priority to increase business for the destination, perhaps at specific times of the year. To this end, you should carefully analyse the profile of Internet users, market by market, in relation to your target market segments. This will guide you on the extent to which the Internet will be an effective distribution channel.

Specifying the Web Site Functionality

As a first stage in specifying the functionality you require from your own Web site, it is worthwhile spending time looking at other destination sites and learning from them. Look at the information on Web sites in the previous chapter and then take a look at those that seem to relate to your own objectives. Decide which features you would like to include in your site and what are the weaknesses to be avoided. Think carefully about what consumers in your different priority market segments might require from the site.

In specifying functionality for your own site, the features you should consider should include the following:

- 'Findability' – making the site easy to find through an obvious URL (Web site address) or search engines

- Speed – ensuring the site operates quickly, with options to not load graphics for users with slow machines

- Design – making the site attractive and easy to use, so that it holds the user's interest

- Content – providing content that is current, accurate, relevant, and sufficiently detailed; using video, animation and images in a controlled way to enhance effectiveness, without detracting seriously from performance

- Searchability – helping users to find what they require easily, through search facilities with appropriate criteria and navigable maps with zoom

- Bookability – making it easy to check availability, book and/or pay for products and services on line, with assured security

- Links – providing links to other sites, reciprocated to allow easy return and exploiting third party relationships to deliver useful content, such as travel information

- Customisation – recognising customers who have visited the site before and providing information to meet their known requirements

- Help – providing help to navigate the site and/or get help with queries about the content or booking

- Enquiry response – providing an efficient mechanism for handling booking enquiries, where online booking is not available.

Once you have a reasonable idea of what functionality you require on your own site, you can start work on preparing a functional specification. This will form the basis of your tender document and should describe your objectives, the features you require in your site and the way you expect it to work.

Preparation of a Structure and Design

Once you have your functional specification drafted it is time to bring in technical skills. The structure and design of the site will depend on:

(a) business factors:

- the size of your destination and the number of individual products to be promoted

- the anticipated frequency of updating the information

- the order in which the products should be displayed - alphabetical, randomised, etc

- whether secure online transactions are required

- the amount of customer data required

(b) technical factors

- the relative importance of the search engines for users in finding the site

- whether to host your own Web server or buy the service from an Internet Service Provider

- the generation of browser predominant in the target markets – third generation browsers impose considerably more constraints than fourth generation

- the level of screen resolution to be accommodated.

If you anticipate promoting more than (say) fifty individual tourism products and/or you wish to update the information on a regular basis, then you should build your Web Site so that it can be database driven. This will involve using Active Server Pages (ASP), where each page is a template with data dynamically delivered into pre-programmed areas each time the page is activated.

The alternative, 'hard-coding' the information in HTML, is viable for a very simple site, but would be too restrictive for sites where there are regular developments and changes to the data.

Make sure your technical and content people liaise at the early stages. They should work together to develop a navigation chart which shows the relationship between all the screens, and how one leads to another, together with the screen solutions which show the layout and graphic design of each page.

You need to strike a balance between a desire for full multimedia material to stimulate interest and promote the destination and the need to maintain a high standard of performance by the site. Users will not want to wait five minutes while a graphic downloads, no matter how good the quality. Simple and quick is much better than creative and slow.

In terms of your original objectives, if you need to raise awareness of your destination, then you will need more editorial information and less product information. If your objective is to provide a booking mechanism for existing demand, the site needs to be quick and easy for the customer to identify what they want and book it – for example, Travelocity's "Three clicks to book".

It is possible to create different URLs for different uses, so that you can bring users in at the appropriate point in the site. This is often achieved by putting an extension on the URL – for example, www.holland.com/book.

The design team will develop a look and feel for the site (reflecting the corporate style of the destination if one exists). In doing this they should bear in mind the following points:

- Keep the site simple and easy to use. Try to avoid a lot of clutter – potentially a problem if you are incorporating advertising.

- Many search engines find framed areas within the screen difficult to handle and may ignore sites with this feature – but note that this is less of an issue with the latest browsers, Netscape 5 and above.

- Do not to use a large number of scrollable pages. It is easier for the user if everything is in view on the page.

- Be careful with font types and sizes and the use of coloured text. Carry out some user trials to ensure all text is easy to read, and remember that text changes colour once you have viewed that item.

- There is a growing convention for left-hand navigation, which you may or may not wish to adopt

- If you are linking with other sites, consider doing this within a window of your site, so you do not lose your customer.

Contracting an Agency

It is likely that you will want to buy in some services from a agencies that might be concerned with such issues as brand development, advertising, systems development, etc. Depending on the capacity of your own team you can buy in services to:

- Work with you to develop the brand, look and feel of your destination

- Work with you to develop the functional specification of your site

- Develop the technical specification

- Build the site

- Organise the data collection and input of the stock

- Host and maintain the site on your behalf

- Project manage the implementation

- Register the site with the search engines and maintain a good ranking with them

- Provide analysis of users and their usage of the site.

The more specific you can be in your brief to agencies, the easier it is for them to price the job. You may wish to work with just one agency that can deliver all the services you need, or with several, each carrying out a specialist task. The latter is perfectly feasible, but will require you to ensure co-operation, with the dependencies between agencies clearly identified and documented - and penalties included in the contract where time is critical.

In order to decide on an agency, identify potential candidates and find out as much as you can about their capabilities. Ask to see a sample of their portfolio and speak to some of their existing clients in order to obtain a reference. This should enable you to draw up a short list for tender.

If you want an agency to help you with the project in the first instance, let the contract in small stages so that you are not tied into a long-term deal before you understand what is really required. For instance, you may want to engage an agency to help you draft a functional and technical specification and then ask them to tender to build the site. A third party could host and maintain the server and provide analysis for you.

If you intend to update the data regularly it would be sensible to take the work in-house, as far as possible. This offers a far higher degree of flexibility and enables you to react quickly to emerging opportunities.

Once you have decided to which agency(ies) you will award the contract, you will need to draw up formal service level agreements. These should include a detailed project plan, with milestones and targets, the dependencies carefully documented, and a delivery and payment schedule. Include penalty clauses for suppliers who fail to deliver on time or to the required standard, especially if this impacts on other suppliers. Be sure to build in some contingency, in terms of both time and budget. It is more than likely that there will be problems along the way.

Beware of specification creep - adding more features after you have begun work. Try to finalise the specification and the contracts before work starts. Draw up a formal change control procedure, so that changes can be accommodated in an orderly way, with both parties aware of the time and cost implications.

Origination of Product Information in Digital Form

You may already have a considerable number of product resources, transparencies, prints, video and slides, which can be processed into digital form relatively easily. Keeping such 'imageware' in digital form is a far more effective way of storing, cataloguing and retrieving it than if it were in a physical form. However, there will be a cost, so consider carefully what you really will use.

Several issues need to be considered when digitising existing resources:

- The required resolution of imageware (images used for small scale pictures on-screen need only be scanned at 72dpi, whereas images to be output as print need a much higher resolution.)

- The same image often needs to be scanned and then saved at several different sizes and resolutions

- Video for the Web needs to be compressed and reduced to 256 colours

- A nomenclature needs to be developed which is consistent and logical

- Care should be taken to ensure copyright and data protection rules are adhered to

- Text data need to be input against common terminology standards

Digital cameras have made the origination of product information in digital form a relatively easy job. (Of course, it should not be assumed that just because someone can operate a digital camera, that they can take a good photograph. The skills of a professional are still required to direct a photo shoot and ensure that the content of the picture is as good as the technical output.)

Text based product information can be originated in several ways:

- Imported from legacy databases

- Through manual input by a keyboard and mouse

- By optical scanning of forms

- By touch tone telephony

- By voice recognition.

Again care needs to be taken to ensure the quality of the data.

Production of Editorial and Graphical Material

Most DMOs want to have an image and content rich Web site, but care needs to be taken to ensure that lengthy download times do not impair the performance of the site. Video clips should be used sparingly as should plug-ins and animations. Use still pictures with fade and change animation effects to save space and time.

Digital cameras and modern software offer a vast array of features to help you take advantage of the multimedia nature of the Web. Panoramic 360° views, zooms and animations can all be accommodated, but take care that such features do not distract your user from the main message.

The use of sound files with other features can sometimes cause difficulties. Video clips generally have sound files incorporated within them, so are reasonably easy to accommodate. Separate sound files running together with silent video or change animations can sometimes be difficult to achieve without stilted pauses or the screen going momentarily black. Improvements to software specifications should solve this problem in the future.

Provide maps to help your users orientate themselves, having regard to copyright laws. If you need to show your tourism products located on a map graphic, this can be done dynamically from the database using map references, or through Geographic Information System (GIS) technology.

Users do not enjoy reading large amounts of text on-screen so make sure your editorial is punchy, maintains interest and gets over the essential points without becoming too long.

Testing/Evaluation of Pilot Site

Ensure that your agency builds a trial version of your site, and has sufficient sample data to allow you to thoroughly test the system. Every combination of search criteria needs to be tested at least three times.

First you must test and accept the software. You will need to:

- Draw up a software acceptance plan against which you will test the system and sign it off as acceptable

- Draw up a 'bug sheet' on which you will note any failures

- Test each function at least three times to ensure the system returns the expected result

- Regenerate the database and carry out the same tests to ensure they 'stick'

- Make some changes and test again

- Regenerate and test again

- Ensure the 'black box' data is being properly recorded

- Test that the processes for transferring files to the Web server work properly

- Test that all links to and from third party sites work correctly

- Once you have completed the acceptance plan, you will have a number of bug sheets detailing the failure points, these should be sent to the developer

- Do not assume that everything will be fixed in one go. Carry out rigorous regression testing, to cater for the situation where the correcting of one fault leads to failures in functionality that was working properly previously.

Secondly you must validate the data. You will need to:

- Proof read all the data carefully for spelling mistakes and typing mistakes

- Check the data for accuracy, include some form of validation check by the owner of the data

- Carry out some random checks to independently verify that the data you have been given is correct.

Thirdly you must validate the business processes, where relevant. You will need to:

- Carry out some sample transactions

- Ensure all the necessary response mechanisms are in place

- Put in a system for handling complaints.

Once these stages are complete, move on to a full testing, by revealing your site to business colleagues who understand tourism and have some experience of the Web. Ask them to evaluate the site, including transactions, and then provide you with comments on areas for improvement.

Ideally you should identify some independent users (perhaps students at a local University) and ask them to undertake the same process. It is more valuable if they are not experienced Web users, as this will reveal any weaknesses in your design structure.

Once these stages are complete, you can incorporate any changes into the site and revalidate the software.

Implementation, Monitoring and Evaluation

Once you are happy that your site is sufficiently tested to be used by the public, you should publish the URL and register it with the major search engines.

At first you will probably achieve high ratings on the search engines (assuming, of course, that you have paid careful attention to the design of the site). However, the way the systems work means that your position will soon start to slip and you will have to take positive steps to ensure you maintain a reasonable position. The search engines are continuously reviewing their policies for ranking, so you have to be alert to know what action you must take.

Once your site is implemented you need to spend time analysing its performance, in terms of:

- the robustness of the site (i.e. monitoring down-time)

- its position in the search engines listings

- the number of users of designated pages of the site

- the amount of business it is generating.

A key feature of the Internet is that users leave an electronic footprint that is a powerful aid to marketing. It is possible to obtain a wide range of information about users - where they are from, what time of day they visited, how long they stayed, what they looked at and what they bought, but the complexity of the data means that you must interpret it with care.

If time and resources permit, correspond with users who provide feedback to gain a deeper understanding about them and their needs, to supplement the statistical data.

There are several other ways of monitoring the performance of your site:

- To encourage users to register their details, provide incentives, such as a special offer, a quiz or a free-draw – for example: "Tell us the top 10 things you like about Spain for a chance to win a free weekend in Madrid".

- Set up a newsgroup or chat room

- Provide feedback forms

- Correspond by e-mail whenever possible

- Track the amount of business being generated

- Gather information from linked sites about the number of 'click-throughs' they have received.

Promoting the Use of your Web Site

There are three major ways to promote your Web site:

Promote the URL

This is often referred to as 'drive to Web'. It involves publicising your URL so potential customers can log straight onto your site. You can use different gateway pages to help you track where the user found out about you, or bring customers into the site at the pages that specifically interest them.

You have many opportunities to publicise your URL and it should be promoted as widely as your phone number. Print it on all your brochures, stationery, corporate material, promotional literature and in your advertising. Try to adopt a URL that reflects your destination name, something easy to remember like www.visitbritain.co.uk.

Obtain Links from other Sites

It is important to establish links from other Web sites to generate business for your site. This can often be arranged on a reciprocal basis at no cost; in some circumstances, however, you will have to pay a fee. Also, you should consider establishing partnerships with other organizations that can provide required content cost effectively – for example, with a motoring organization to provide traffic information or with organizations that provide weather forecasts.

Similarly you can offer links to the sites of your providers from the relevant pages on your site. This may well provide an opportunity for you to generate income for your DMO. These kind of arrangements usually provide a win/win situation for both organizations, but you should take care to review all proposed linked sites to ensure that they will add value to your site, not detract from it.

You may wish to purchase advertising on third party Web sites – for example, the search engines or the online travel agencies. Banner advertising is popular but rates vary enormously; you are usually charged a fee per view, ie. each time the advert is displayed. Fees range from $25 per thousand views (CPM) upwards.

Many of the search engine providers and ISPs offer a registration facility so that you may register your site in particular categories of their directories. This is usually free and can provide a useful promotional platform, as these home sites tend to have large volumes of traffic.

Search Engines

If your destination is large or well known, you will probably be less reliant on the search engines, particularly if you have an appropriate URL, such as www.visitchile.com. In this case you stand a good chance of being found by users guessing your URL. Destinations that are less well known or have limited resources, may find the search engines particularly helpful. However, the resources required to keep your site at the top of the search engine listings should not be underestimated. The search engines are constantly changing the criteria they use to rank sites. They have independent editors reviewing sites, but the sheer number of sites being added each day means that much of their work is done automatically. You need to ensure your agency has a full understanding of the workings of the major search engines when they design your site.

Critical Success Factors

Listed below are the factors considered critical to the success of Web site development and promotion:

- Ensure the message and content of your site is appropriate to your target audience

- Create a lively design, which maintains interest throughout the site, and reflects the nature of your destination and your DMO's corporate or promotional style

- Ensure the functionality of your site meets your business objectives, such as awareness raising, information provision, transaction processing. Pay constant attention to new user requirements and customer expectations

- Develop partnerships and links with third parties (e.g. transport operators, mail order retailers) to help deliver content and/or provide a response/sales support mechanism

- Ensure your content is current and accurate and that third party information published on your site maintains a similarly high standard

- Do not compromise performance in order to exploit multimedia features

- Invest in the promotion of your URL and ensure you can be found easily by the major search engines

- Test the site thoroughly before launching it

- Monitor its performance, evaluate your results and make any amendments on a regular basis

This next list details the critical success factors for proactive electronic marketing, going beyond the development and implementation of a Web site:

- Build a customer database and capture as much information as you can about the lifestyle, travel and buying habits of your customers

- Develop and nurture a one-to-one relationship with your customers. Communicate by e-mail wherever possible, as it is personal and immediate, but less intrusive than the telephone

- Use database-filtering tools to ensure that proactive mailshots are really personal.

- Use competitions, auctions, chat rooms, feedback forms, quizzes to encourage your customers to tell you more about themselves

- Tailor your product offering more exactly to fit the demands of your customers

- Give your customers a reason to come back to your Web site and encourage them to buy on impulse.

DEVELOPING A DESTINATION MANAGEMENT SYSTEM

The programme of work involved in developing a Web site (as outlined above) may appear complicated and demanding. However, it is relatively straightforward compared with the process of specifying, designing and implementing a Destination Management System. This is complex because, as explained previously, DMSs are designed today to be the infrastructure for the integrated DMO, supporting multiple functions from core databases.

The main components of a DMS are:

- The technical infrastructure of computers and network hardware and software

- The database management system (DBMS), together with the software required to manage and access the data in the DBMS

- The applications software that undertakes the functions to support the business activities

- The data content.

These components necessarily interrelate and must be looked at in parallel in the planning process.

To provide meaningful advice on the process of specifying, designing and implementing such systems would require a separate handbook. However, as initial guidance, the process might involve the following ten steps:

1. Prepare a draft strategic overview - a short document setting out the context (particularly the strategy for market and industry development) and the organization's business need for a DMS.

2. Advise and consult key partners (e.g. transport carriers, tour operators, entertainment and events organisers, telecom companies, credit card companies, etc.), stakeholders and staff, to gain their support for an initiative that will require a substantial investment of money and staff time and have a major impact on the way that the DMO works.

3. Prepare a draft specification of user requirements. To this end, construct a list of the future business activities and processes that you wish to be supported by the DMS; and decide what tasks you want the technology to perform (the 'functionality') and the level of priority you attach to each.

4. Build up your knowledge of systems on the market by issuing to the suppliers a Request for Information (RFI) incorporating the specification of user requirements; and by going to see the systems in operation.

5. Based on your increased knowledge, and with specialist advice where necessary, finalise the strategic overview, extend the specification of requirements to become a Functional Specification and prepare the initial business case analysis, incorporating both financial and non-financial costs and benefits.

6. Request and evaluate tender(s). The functional specification, together with the specification of user requirements, should be used as the basis of a Request for Proposals (RFP), to obtain formal tenders – recognising the possibility that you may wish to buy components from different suppliers and integrate them.

7. Obtain a technical specification, including the 'network architecture' and agree procurement programme.

8. Undertake a full business case analysis, now that the scope and costs of the project finalised, you may wish to revisit and revise the analysis, possibly as the basis for the final decision to proceed with the project.

9. Prepare an implementation plan, including a critical path analysis, in conjunction with the lead supplier. It should cover not only the installation of the IT itself, but everything that the DMO itself will have to do as an integral part of the programme.

10. Set up a steering group to drive and monitor implementation.

In implementing a DMS of any significant scale, there must be a Project Manager to act on behalf of the DMO and a clear structure (see Step 10 above) to enable and assist the Project Manager to report to and interact with all the sections of the DMO. The Project Manager's job is to direct the DMS project in order to support the DMO's strategy and business objectives, and to ensure that both the client and the supplier(s) deliver their sides of the contract. Ideally the Project Manager should be involved (at least part-time) from the early stages of the project and possibly undertake most of the planning work involved.

DMS Critical Success Factors

1. To have the best chance of success, a DMS should be integral to the operations of a DMO or a partnership of DMOs, and should be business-led, not technology-led.

2. Setting up a DMS is not a 'once and for all' cost. There will be substantial revenue costs and additional capital costs on a continuing basis. Prepare business case analysis (BCA) projections over three or four years. Undertake an initial BCA early on, and a more detailed one later, when you have a clearer idea of the proposition and the costs.

3. It is unlikely that in the short term a DMS will pay for itself financially. Do not assume that there will immediately be a large increase in income.

4. Implementation of a full DMS should be phased in over a similar time period, starting by setting up the internal network, getting staff used to using the latest office software, e-mailing, etc. A number of small steps is a lot easier to take than 'one giant leap'.

5. Staff understanding, buy-in and involvement is essential and requires specific programmes of consultation, discussion and active participation, backed up by appropriate training and development activity, including change management programmes. It is important to ensure in this way that the pressures that can be caused by setting up a DMS and by implementing new ways of working do not become de-motivating.

6. When dealing with system suppliers, be sceptical and make sure to ask the key questions. Remember that it is a realistic possibility to purchase different

components of the DMS from different suppliers, although interface problems can arise.

7. Go for proven, off-the-shelf software, wherever possible. Where it is necessary to develop new software, remember that a substantial investment of DMO staff time will be needed to work with the software developer; and the process may be a long one.

8. Where deadlines are critical, include penalty clauses in supplier contracts.

9. Achieving and maintaining a high quality digital database is a substantial task, for which proper resources should be allowed.

10. Set up a mechanism to drive implementation and to monitor and evaluate progress openly and honestly against deadlines and budgets.

PURCHASING TRAVEL IN THE INFORMATION AGE

Travel and tourism are here to stay. In 25 or 50 years' time, we will still enjoy travelling to new destinations for recreation and vacation. No one believes that travel and tourism will be replaced by a virtual experience. Tourists will still seek the adventure and excitement of visiting new places. However, by then we will be many years into the Information Age and, what started as a revolution in the 1990s at the end of the Second Millennium, will be a natural way of life.

Supermarkets will have closed their branches many years ago. They will operate efficient online sales channels, supported by centralised warehouse logistics operations. The first supermarket chains are already trialling this business model and online bookstores such as Amazon.com, have built there entire businesses around online ordering and fast, centralised, delivery operations. Banks will no longer have branches. They will offer electronic online banking services supported by centralised call centre support. By this time, society will be predominantly cashless. Money will still exist but cash will be carried on a smart card, a credit card sized card with an embedded micro-chip. Credit card companies have already run extensive trials with electronic purses in the form of smart cards.

In 25 years time, consumers will purchase and receive delivery of information products exclusively online. When they buy travel, an information product at the point of sale, they will not dream of leaving their homes or offices to walk into high street retail premises that cannot even physically demonstrate the product, let alone provide any more information than they can access on their net appliances.

Older consumers will remember the last few years of the Second Millennium and realise that this was the period when the Information Age began. They will remember that travel and tourism, more than any other industry, contributed to a new way of life. They will know that, during that exciting period of change, the travel industry showed the world that electronic distribution is the preferred way of retailing.

Within the next couple of years, expect to see computers without keyboards that understand the human voice sufficiently well that there is no need for a manual input device. As Internet service providers and telecommunications providers increase the bandwidth of their networks (ie. increase the amount of data they can carry), expect to see video phones come into more common use. As more satellites are launched, expect to see increasing use of mobile communications. Even within the house, the "wired " telephone will become an item of the past.

How will consumers shop for travel and tourism products? In any way that they want! Consider the following diagram. This is the traditional model of travel distribution. For simplification purposes, it just illustrates airline travel but is equally applicable to all travel products.

In the model, the consumer books a flight either directly with the airline or contacts a travel agent who facilitates the transaction. Contact with the agent is via the telephone or face-to-face. The agent books with the airline directly or via a computer interface with a GDS.

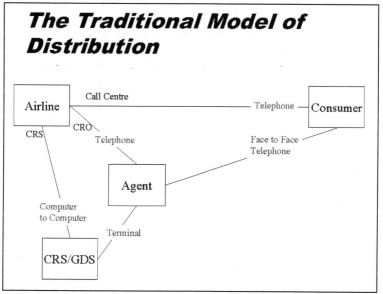

Source: Genesys – The Travel Technology Consultancy

The next diagram shows how distribution is developing. It is the Multi-Channel Model of Distribution. Note that the travel agent and travel principal, in this case the airline, are connected to the consumer by a whole array of different distribution channels. Instead of the consumer considering which airline or agent to contact, he or she is now more interested in the convenience of the channel.

As consumers become accustomed to instant information retrieval and online e-commerce facilities so they will care less about who they are purchasing from and be more concerned about using the most convenient channel. At the office the consumer may prefer using the Web from his/her PC. At home interactive digital television may be more convenient. When out and about he or she will wish to use a mobile telephony device. Even now, several mobile telephone networks are launching Internet connectivity.

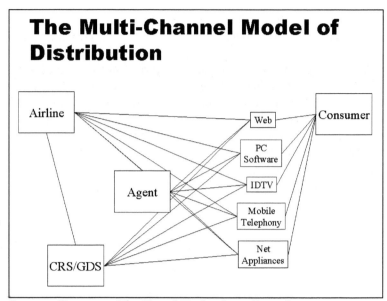

Source: Genesys – The Travel Technology Consultancy

Travel and tourism companies will come under increasing pressure to provide seamless distribution, ie. enable customers to make contact in whichever way they desire. This entails having information systems that provide a single view of product and customer databases both to in-house staff and to those who are retrieving information online. Seamless distribution can be embodied in three "musts":

1. The customer **must** be recognised.

2. Information on current transactions **must** be available.

3. Any actions required **must** be achievable.

For destination marketing organizations that may have offices all over the world and may not be connected to centralised databases, this is a major challenge.

Intelligent Agents

The search engines and directories of today such as Yahoo! or Excite are not intelligent tools. They have vast databases. The largest - Northern Light - has currently indexed 155 million Web pages. They are able to filter keyword searches in an efficient manner but require significant human management and intervention. Users need to carefully consider how best to initiate searches to yield the best results.

This can be contrasted with the goal of intelligent agent technology, which is to introduce software that will apply some reasoning and processing to the task required by its user. Early examples included a trial Web site for CD shopping. The user could simply enter the title of a CD and the agent software would visit several online vendors gathering prices and availability. All the user had to do was to browse this information, choose a preferred vendor and go directly to the appropriate Web site to complete the transaction. It would, of course, be technically feasible for the intelligent agent software to complete the transaction on behalf of its user.

Consider the following diagram showing the process flow of a hypothetical intelligent agent that can shop for flights. The agent would carry out the following actions:

1. It would allow the user, the traveller, to specify his or her preferred flight requirements. This would include the obvious parameters of dates and times, departure and destination points, preferred airlines and class. It might also include seating preferences, aisle or window. As the agent is capable of purchasing on behalf of the user, the preferences might also include parameters regarding financial arrangements. For example, the user might specify a rule that the agent should just report on what is available but if there is a fare available that is at least $20 less than the next lowest, the agent should make the purchase without further instruction.

2. Without any further involvement from the user, the agent would go online and search airline and agency Web sites, gathering the information it needs to make a decision on whether to purchase.

3. If the agent found a fare within its user's financial parameters to purchase, it would do so. If not, it would simply report. Note in the diagram that the agent has purchased and the ticket is in the post. With the widespread adoption of E-Ticketing where there is not physical document to be delivered, it will be even more convenient to utilise software agents for purchasing travel.

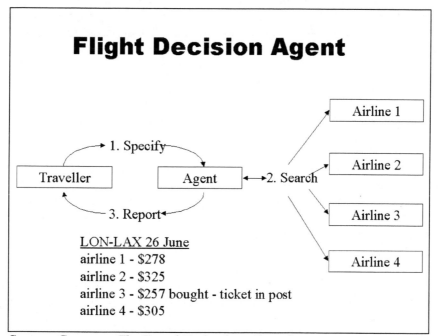

Source: Genesys – The Travel Technology Consultancy

In fact, the implications of using intelligent agent technology for consumer transactions are much farther reaching than just saving users the time to do the task themselves.

Imagine now, a scenario envisioned by developers of this technology wherein agents will be able to collude on behalf of their owners. In the hypothetical case above, the agent was making a single purchase on behalf of its owners. The agent, knowing its owner's requirements, might then seek out other agents which have been instructed to make the same purchase. They could then form a purchasing group and make a powerful case for offering a bulk purchase discount. The agents, as a group, could negotiate on behalf of their owners. In this way, the shopping power of the individual could be radically increased.

We are looking at a scenario where the ability to control price is shifted from the vendor to the purchaser. This is happening now, even before intelligent agent technology becomes a reality, with the advent of auction Web sites. These invite consumers to make a bid for products, price being driven by the rules of supply and demand.

Buyer Driven Commerce

With the rapid growth of the Internet, for the first time we can allow buyers to tell sellers what they want to purchase and how much they want to pay. This is the business philosophy of buyer driven commerce. The technology that sits behind this is a demand collection system which harvests a demand from each customer and presents their offers to suppliers, which then pick and choose what offers to fulfil.

All sellers maximise profits by matching price and inventory. It is easy to sell everything at one low price and it is also easy to sell a few things at a much higher price. But it is hard to sell the most at the best price. This is particularly so in travel where the product is perishable. Once a flight has taken off with empty seats, these can never be filled. However, in the airline and hotel business, sellers stop selling to the leisure customers in order to hold on to seats and rooms that yield higher prices from their business customers. This may result in having to dispose of excess capacity which typically means selling at the wrong price.

If an airline marks down its excess capacity for clearance, full price sales can be adversely effected. If the unsold seats are sold to a consolidator, the airline may not be maximising its own revenue. Cutting price is frequently used as a tactic by travel companies to move unsold inventory but it positions the product as a commodity, training consumers to wait before buying on the basis that they are more likely to get a bargain. With the GDS distribution that provides consumers with near perfect information, anybody through their travel agent or directly on the Internet, can quickly find what prices are available for a similar product and they will objectively assess competing value propositions.

An organization called Priceline.com has designed and implemented a solution to the problem of having to markdown prices to move inventory, one that is fully automated and enables sellers to ask and receive an answer to a question that they have never been able to ask customers. What are you willing to pay and what trade-offs are you willing to make? The answer to the question can generate a real transaction. At Priceline.com's Web site, visitors make offers to purchase travel products and these are guaranteed by a credit card. The potential buyers commit to buy if any qualified seller agrees to their price. The demand collection system is authorised by the buyer to transact if the seller agrees to the offer. It becomes a guaranteed sale and the transaction, once complete, is irrevocable.

This business model has worked well for Priceline.com who now sell between 3,000 and 4,000 flight tickets per day for over 20 participating airlines. It also provides valuable statistics as the entire spectrum of demand is visible above and below the price at which the airline is willing to sell. Of course, when buyers name their own price, they need not only offer the lowest possible amount. If a product is in demand, then buyers may offer to pay more than a supplier might have otherwise priced a product. Demand collection systems are facilitating the sale of products priced on the basis of supply and demand creating marketplaces where the buyer and the seller are both winners.

The Role of Smart Cards

A smart card is a credit card that has embedded within it a micro-chip. This can be used to store data relating to the card holder in a way that is far more secure than the magnetic stripe found on most credit cards. Moreover, the micro-chip can hold far more data than a magnetic strip and "compartmentalise" this, ie. place data relating to different applications into separate areas of its memory.

Many believe that smart cards have a key role to play in the future of global travel. For example, MasterCard, which is involved in the development of smart card applications, currently captures in excess of $110 billion of worldwide expenditure on travel and entertainment and estimates that by the year 2002 this sector will surpass retail to become the segment with the largest spend (over $2 trillion).

Smart card solutions have already been implemented by travel and transport organizations. Airlines such as Lufthansa and American Airlines allow frequent travellers to check-in and board using a smart card for identification. Hilton Hotels in partnership with American Express offer self check-in and check-out.

A future scenario for advocates of smart cards is one where the traveller carries just one card that fulfils all his or her needs for identification, ticketing and payments. This might result in the following scenario:

Making the Booking
- Log on to online booking service. View options available in line with company travel policy and individual entitlements.
- Select and compile full travel itinerary.
- Send order.
- Download to card: e-ticket, hotel reservation, car rental.
- Download to card: cash from online ATM to electronic purse on card.
- Check travel insurance details on card.

Transport to Airport
- Pay taxi using electronic purse on card.

At the Airport
- Check-in with e-ticket held on card, update loyalty points.
- Gain access to executive lounge using card as the key.
- Board plane and use card to access on-board systems facilities.

Arrive at Destination
- Card acts as passport, holding all the immigration and visa information required.

Collect Rental Car
- Card holds driving licence and insurance details.

Check-in at Hotel
- Card allows reservation confirmation and self check-in.
- Card is validated for use as a room key.
- Card is used to access systems facilities in the room.
- Card is used for checking-out.

Back at the Office
- Details of the trip are downloaded from the card to a PC for transfer to an expense management system.

Whilst, the above scenario describes a business trip, smart card technology is also applicable to leisure travel and tourism. Many of the above applications would still be valid but there are also additional areas where smart cards can bring benefits without the card having to be all encompassing. For example, in urban and regional transport: several train and bus organizations are trialling or using smart card electronic purses as a convenient method payment. Card holders can charge a value to their cards away from the ticket office and then have no need to queue to purchase a ticket. Journey costs are automatically deducted from the card as the holder exits a station or terminal. Because cards are not tickets that are only valid on one type of transport they are ideal for inter-modal transport, allowing users to board buses, trains and ferries with ease. All that is required is for the transport companies to agree on a common standard of card.

Resort organizations such as Club Med have adopted smart card style electronic purses for use in resort, so obviating the need for their guests to carry money. Similar electronic purse trials have been operated in a number of areas of the world such as Jersey in the Channel Islands. The convenience of carrying a card instead of currency is compelling. Banks and other financial institutions are agreeing on standards that will allow card holders to transfer money to their smart cards over the telephone. Over the coming years, expect to see telephones and PCs equipped with smart card readers for this purpose.

The argument for the introduction of globally accepted smart cards is compelling. Just one concern will always remain. The more dependent people become on smart cards to facilitate global travel arrangements, the greater the personal crisis when a card goes astray.

CHAPTER 7: CONCLUSIONS

INTRODUCTION

The Internet has ushered in the Information Age, an era of sweeping change that will leave no business or industry untouched. It took radio 30 years to reach 90 million people. Television took 15 years to achieve the same penetration. The Internet has achieved this in just three years and its rate of growth continues to accelerate.

Some estimate that as many as 400,000 companies and organizations now have Web sites and are on-sale globally with Jupiter Communications forecasting that the online consumer travel industry will be worth $16.6 billion by 2003. Bearing in mind that tourism receipts in 1998 were $445 billion (excluding air travel) and are projected to grow, this may seem a small amount. However, consumers habits are changing as they enter the Information Age. A recent survey by NFO Interactive, conducted in May 1999, found that just over 24% of consumers who are already shopping online expect to spend less purchasing goods in high street retail shops and more online in the next six months. The fact is that consumers are already taking to shopping online and every organization within the travel and tourism industry must take account of this and plan accordingly.

During any period of change, there are winners and losers. The winners will be those travel and tourism organizations that can adapt to the new way of doing business in the Information Age. The losers will be those that think there is no need to change. The Winners and Losers section in this chapter reviews the reasoning behind the forecasts of who will come out on top and who may be forced out of business.

There is no doubt that destination marketing organizations will change in the Information Age. They may find new roles and may participate in the take-up of tourism products in a way that may currently seem alien.

There is no reason why tourism organizations should not reap the benefits of the Information Age. Imagine a time in the not too distant future when there is no longer any need to produce expensive, printed marketing literature. All that is needed is one electronic copy that is available to the world's tourists via the Internet. Imagine a time when DMOs no longer need a network of national tourist offices within the major outbound markets of the world. All that is needed is a centralised organization that is online to the world.

The Information Age promises a vision for a new way of life.

THE WINNERS AND LOSERS

The travel and tourism industry is one that has more intermediaries than other industries. These are the tour operators and travel agents that package and distribute products on behalf of travel principals such as hotelliers and airlines. It could be argued that a DMO also acts as an intermediary, feeding tourists with information on products available within its destination. However, until recently, the traditional DMO had no financial interest in the contract between the tourist and the seller of travel prodcuts. This is starting to change and is examined in the section below which discusses opportunities for public and private partnership.

New Strategic Threats

The introduction of new technology is creating a number of strategic threats to the continued success of intermediaries, particularly travel agents, who often add no more value to a travel transaction than to facilitate the booking. A useful framework to analyse these threats is Michael Porter's Model for Structural Analysis which was first published in 1980 in his book entitled "Competitive Strategy".

The model places the business in the centre of its market and competitive environment, as the following diagram illustrates:

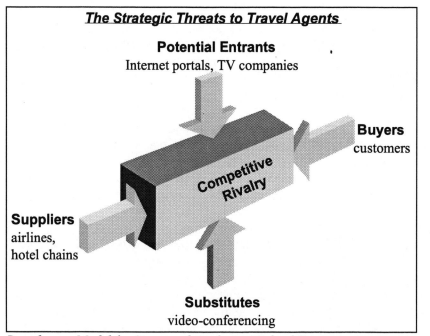

Based upon Model for Structural Analysis, Michael Porter

From the diagram, it can be seen that there are five areas of strategic threat to travel intermediaries. The new technology of the Information Age has caused these threats to increase.

Competitive Rivalry

There has always been intense competition in the travel industry and this is usually price led, with intermediaries marketing their products on price. This is in spite of the fact that travel is a clearly differentiated product. However, when travel and tourism industry players wish to boost sales they do not stress the value added features of their products, but compete by price cutting and discounting. In this manner, some market segments of the industry treat its product as a commodity. Travellers have come to understand this and will shop on price. Technology is a great enabler of this. For example, for many years now the neutral displays of the airline GDSs have price at the forefront of the purchase decision by ranking flights by price. Following, is an example of how one online travel agent, Internet Holidays, is representing mass market, standardised leisure travel products. Notice that the only details provided are date, destination and price. To choose a holiday, the user clicks on price.

Economic theory predicts that there can only be one cost winner, just one business that has achieved sufficient economies of scale that it can undercut all its rivals. It can then afford to price lower and drive its competitors out of business. As travel companies grow larger and distribution technology increases market perfection, allowing travellers to shop globally with ease, so smaller and less efficient travel companies will fall by the wayside.

Survivors in the new world of electronic travel markets would not just be those with the lowest cost operations, but also smaller companies that have moved away from competitive rivalry by specialising, ie. by adopting niche marketing strategies and so clearly differentiating their products and services. The message for DMOs is that they should endeavour to position their destinations as unique products, unlike any other and so move away from competing purely on cost.

Buyers

The previous sections reviewing developments in intelligent agent technology and buyer driven commerce, clearly described how the power of the customer to bargain will increase. The travel industry is moving slowly towards accepting auctioning techniques to move distressed stocks and this is another step towards providing the customer with the ultimate power to dictate price.

Suppliers

Travel principals, the suppliers to the industry, are placing intermediaries under intense pressure. Airlines, in particular, have introduced aggressive commission capping that limits the amount of money an agent will earn by selling a flight. There is also a new generation of direct sell suppliers that are using the Internet to sell to the traveller, without having any inclination to distribute via intermediaries. All travel principals must have it in mind that the Internet is a viable distribution channel that can allow them to cut the intermediary out of the equation.

Potential Entrants

As will have been seen in Chapter 4, new online distribution mechanisms have allowed new entrants to penetrate the travel marketplace. There are no longer any geographic barriers to entry and organizations, such as Expedia, that have built a body of online travel retailing experience in the United States are now moving into the United Kingdom and Europe.

Portals are also establishing themselves as purveyors of travel. They own the distribution relationship and are seeking to leverage this by selling goods and services. Travel is ideal for this as it is an electronic product.

Substitutes

There is little prospect of a substitute for travel. Video-conferencing has been widely adopted by many companies, being sold as an alternative to business travel. However, experience shows that, in the main, it has created its own niche for meetings that neither warrant a face to face encounter yet require more than a telephone conversation.

The New Electronic Marketplace

There are two major features of the new electronic travel marketplace that will shape the industry and its players, catalysing some organizations to prosper and others to fail.

The first is that consumers are now able to search globally for products that meet their precise needs. There are no longer geographic boundaries protecting the local market. Small travel businesses that served their local communities will find that they are competing head to head with global businesses reaching out across electronic distribution channels right into people's homes. Consumers may find it more convenient to purchase travel on-screen from a company the other side of the world than from their local travel agent in the high street. Niche products such as safaris or mountain trekking that were previously just on-sale within the travel company's local market can now be sold internationally. This means that businesses that may not have been viable selling a specialist travel product in their local market can now exist by cost effectively selling worldwide.

The second feature of the new marketplace is that broad range travel product suppliers will compete on cost and brand power, wielding marketing budgets that keep their brands in the forefront of consumers minds.

With this in mind, the electronic travel marketplace of the Information Age can be encapsulated in the following diagram. It describes travel companies across two attributes. The first is the size of the business – large or small. The second is the focus of the business – is it selling a broad range of travel products or is it specialising, sitting in a niche.

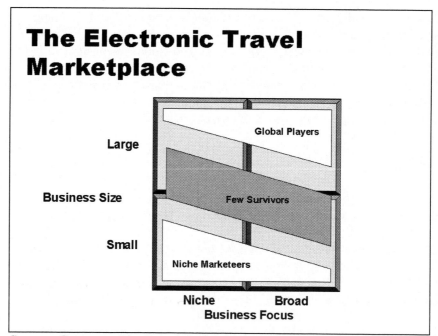

Source: Genesys – The Travel Technology Consultancy

As can be seen from the diagram, the new technologies of the Information Age such as the Internet and interactive digital television will cause the marketplace to polarise. The businesses that will thrive will be either large, global players competing in brand power and economies of scale, or they will be small travel organizations with a clearly focused, specialist product, able to survive because they have little competition and understand their products far better than the global players.

The Losers

The Information Age will cause some travel organizations to fail. These will be:

- Small travel companies who do not adopt a niche. It is clear from the previous analysis that small agents must adopt a specialist product to survive. They will no longer be able to compete by selling any kind of travel product to any kind of traveller. They must meet the challenge by migrating their companies to a new business proposition.

- Medium size companies who are too big to niche market and too small to compete. Few will have the funds to expand to become global players. Most will have a cost base that is too high to allow them to size down to become niche players. Their best hope lies in being acquired and absorbed by a large, multi-national.

- Companies who lose share to the new online businesses and to travel principals. Clearly, the new entrants to the industry and the travel suppliers that will increasingly sell direct are not going to grow the market sufficiently that there will not be casualties. They are going to take market share and drive less efficient travel companies out of business.

- New entrants who do not invest sufficiently in raising and maintaining brand awareness. It is not good enough just to sell travel online. New entrants need to quickly build the brand awareness necessary to convince consumers that they are the people with whom to do business. Faced with similar online travel offerings from agencies with an international reputation, such as American Express and Carlson Wagon Lits, or "New Travel Company Online", most consumers will shop with the former as they are brands that can be trusted.

The Winners

There will be many winners in the Information Age. Organizations that have adapted to the new business rules of the online era. They will be:

- Small travel companies that adapt to offering niche products and services. Many smaller businesses will already be specialists but, for those which are not, it will be difficult to adapt their businesses. However, this is achievable and many small travel organizations will prosper selling products with specialist appeal.

- The global players with high brand awareness, who achieve economies of scale. Perhaps no more than a handful of global travel companies will survive as we move further and further into the Information Age. Those that do, will be extremely efficient organizations who are able to keep their costs to the minimum. They will also be household names, companies that have the brand strength to be trusted.

- New entrants unencumbered by past investment in the high street who already have high brand awareness or who invest in massive marketing campaigns to achieve this. There are currently few non-travel global brands who can compete in the worldwide travel marketplace. One of these is, of course, Microsoft Expedia. There are others who will successfully compete, such as major supermarkets and store chains, who have built an international reputation for retailing and can trade on this to sell travel online. New entrants without this heritage will require deep pockets to fund the marketing campaigns to build brand awareness. For example, Priceline.com raised $100 million for its launch. It spend $80 million of this on its marketing campaign.

- Travel principals who now have a viable direct channel to market and continue to milk the agency channel. The travel principals that divert business away from intermediaries and encourage their customers to book direct are putting profit directly on the bottom line. Commissions that do not have to be paid to agents are pure additional profit. The really successful travel principals are those who are able to build direct channels to the consumer, but continue to have a good relationship with agents until they are no longer needed.

- Global distribution systems who reposition as travel intermediaries. The GDSs can no longer afford to rely upon a business model that positions them as intermediaries between travel agents and travel principals. The successful GDSs will re-position as intermediaries themselves either selling direct to the consumer. Sabre's Travelocity, their online travel agent, is an example of this.

- Technology and software suppliers. More than ever, travel is a technology driven business. Existing technology suppliers and new start-ups are profiting from the industry's thirst for distribution technology solutions.

- Destination marketing organizations. Since their inception, the DMO's main role has been to promote its destination to a worldwide consumer base. This has meant investing huge budgets in the production and distribution of printed media and the maintenance of local offices that can promote and facilitate travel to the destination. The Information Age is heralding an era where cost efficient global marketing and distribution can be taken for granted. Even smaller DMOs that believed they did not previously have the financial muscle to compete on the world stage via traditional channels can now have a global presence. Hopefully, the message from this report is clear: to succeed, emerging DMOs do not necessarily have to command huge budgets. In a new world where sustainable tourism should be the starting point to avoid unnecessary mass market pressures, DMOs have to behave smart and take advantage of the new distribution channels available to them, reaching out to those tourists that provide the most added value.

How DMOs May Evolve

The distribution of travel and tourism products is going through a period of radical change, driven by the opportunities presented by the technology of the Information Age. Tourism authorities and other destination marketing organizations, as an integral part of the industry, can also expect to be affected by change. They will need to embrace new technology to continue to effectively address their primary objective, promoting inbound tourism to their destinations.

Embracing the new technologies of the online world need not be expensive. Every DMO can and should participate but, in doing so and in meeting its objective to promote its destination, the DMO might find its role changing.

This will be driven by the needs of the consumer. In the Information Age, the consumer expects to be able to access comprehensive destination information online whether on a PC screen, via interactive digital television, or a net appliance. Whereas, providing this information may be a satisfactory role for a DMO in 1999, at the start of the Information Age, consumers will quickly expect more. They will expect to transact online, book and reserve the destination products that interest them. The DMOs that wish to encourage inbound tourism to their destinations will need to facilitate bookings and reservations.

The provision of information is a vital role for the DMO but will it be enough? What more can a DMO do? Traditionally, DMOs have provided information and contact details of providers of services such as accommodation. Online, consumers will expect to be able to link to service providers' Web sites to make a booking. In the past, many DMOs have recommended accommodation that they have first quality assured. However, many of these establishments are small businesses that do not have an online presence. Is it within the remit of a DMO to ignore these small businesses that make up such a large proportion of a destination's accommodation stock? Of course not; but agreeing with this statement causes a dilemna. In order to provide a level playing field, the DMO will need to build its own reservation system that can be utilised by these small businesses providing tourism services of all kinds in addition to accommodation.

How will the cost be covered? Relatively few DMOs have the funds to develop and maintain the type of destination management systems (DMS) that provide real time booking facilities for their small accommodation providers. Most DMOs will need to charge a booking transaction fee to help defray the cost of operating their DMS. Is a booking fee fair? Should not those accommodation establishments that have higher room rates pay more? If the answer is yes, then the DMO might decide to charge a commission.

If DMOs are charging commission to accommodation and other service providers within their destination then the DMO is evolving to become an intermediary. The destination marketing organization could be evolving to become the travel agent of the future, a specialist agent that has an in-depth understanding of its product – the destination, travel to, from and within it, and the activities that can be enjoyed whilst there.

Opportunities for Public/Private Partnership

The need for systems integration across public sector DMOs and private sector service providers is catalysing business integration. Some will regard it as inevitable that the DMO will need to enter into partnership with private sector organizations in order to meet its objective of promoting the destination. As will have been noted from the case studies in this report, this is already happening and the trend is growing as the public sector budgets allocated to tourism promotion tend to diminish.

The need to cover the cost of complex, integrated destination management systems has already catalysed many public/private partnerships. Is, therefore, a privately funded, unregulated DMO a feasibility? The experience with Gulliver in Ireland might engender mixed feelings. That when a DMO is operated on the commercial basis of profit maximisation, it must inevitably take sides, working with commercial partners that can offer the best deals whilst ignoring others.

A viable model may be the DMO evolving to act as a travel agent or intermediary for a destination but, as a public organization, being to develop its business in a manner that ensures a fair approach to the private sector service providers that look to it for support. In order to maintain this fairness and offer the widest possible range of destination products, it may have to accept that its funding will not be gained totally from the private sector.

POSSIBLE ROLES FOR THE WORLD TOURISM ORGANIZATION

What role does the World Tourism Organization have to play in facilitating DMOs participation in the Information Age? Sitting at the centre of tourism as it does, the WTO is well suited to develop a number of activities. Some possibilities are reviewed below:

Online Tourism Web Site Directory – As the Internet and the Web continue to grow, it becomes more difficult for users to find Web sites with the information they require. This is leading to a new generation of specialist Web search engines and directories that specialise in particular topics and themes. WTO could assist destination marketing organizations to promote their presence on the Web by developing a specialist search directory which would provide links to DMO Web sites. Links could be ordered geographically by region, so helping visitors to quickly reach the Web sites of destination that interest them. Further possibilities might include offering sorting and searching by activities available within the destination as well as other criteria. WTO could keep this directory exclusive to members or list other DMOs Web sites, possible in return for a fee.

Web Site Approval Mark – When a visitor reaches a Web site, there is usually no confirmation that the information contained therein is accurate and up to date. WTO could operate an approval scheme, allowing those Web sites that have been inspected and that are judged to be of good standard to carry a WTO approval mark. The mark could be designed to convey that the site has met WTO's approval standards. Clicking on the mark could open a small browser window which would explain WTO's approval scheme and why this site can be well regarded.

System Supplier Approval Scheme – The WTO could invite technology suppliers and Web site developers to submit themselves to an audit by WTO. The audit would examine the suppliers' processes and procedures in conducting systems development projects and, providing they reached an acceptable standard, award suppliers with a WTO approval.

Benchmarking Statistics – There is no authority currently benchmarking DMO Web site statistics. WTO could develop a mechanism to regular gather statistics from many DMO Web sites and issue regular bulletins, providing a benchmark by which individual DMOs could judge the success of their own activity on the Web.

Technology Advice – The world of technology can be confusing. One can sometimes receive conflicting advice and one be wary of the vested interest of those providing the information. WTO could offer a technology advisory service, one that members could turn to for impartial and independent advice on matters such as the Web and destination management systems.

Education – As we move into the Information Age, DMOs need to learn about the new techniques and strategies of marketing on the Web. They need to understand how they can take advantage of destination management system technology. WTO could offer educational seminars on these and other technology related topics. The objective would be, not to train DMO managers in the detail of technology, but to provide an understanding of the technologies such that they can plan to take advantage of the new opportunities of the Information Age.

THE FINAL WORD

The technology that is moving the world into the Information Age is providing destination marketing organizations with a cost effective channel through which to reach out across the globe without the high distribution costs of conventional media. Whilst, for many emerging destinations, it may seem that locally there is as yet little interest in the Internet and interactive digital television, the relevant point is that the countries in which the destinations' tourists reside are undoubtedly already embracing these new technologies.

Every DMO can participate online in one form or another and, even if complex destination management systems seem to be beyond feasibility at the present time, every DMO can afford to have a Web site that provides comprehensive and knowledgeable destination information, either by outsourcing the project or managing it in-house.

As we move further into the Information Age, the role of the DMO may change from provider of information and facilitator of tourist/service provider relationships to become one in which the DMO is more commercially involved in tourism transactions. Regardless of this changing role, the DMO must remain the guardian of the destination's interests and main promoter of its worth as a place to be visited. The DMOs objectives must stay aligned with that of the destination and so the model of a fully privatised and commercial DMO is one that may never be successful.

DMO's will remain the primary source of information on the destination and, in order to provide this to consumers and service providers, they will need electronic libraries of text and images that can be conveyed around the world on the digital superhighways of the Internet. DMOs can assist private sector organizations by providing this information in order to promote their destinations.

Every DMO should and can start migrating to the online world. The Information Age is an age of new possibilities for all destinations. It negates the traditional perception that developing countries would never be able to compete on equal terms with developed ones, not having as large budgets to promote their tourism attractions through the costly conventional marketing channels such as the press and television. The Information Age and its associated technology of the Internet is levelling the playing field. All that is required is to grasp the opportunity. We encourage you to follow this challenge.

TECHNICAL GLOSSARY

analogue   - In relation to a television, radio or telephone signal, the older method of conveying data electronically. An analogue signal conveys its information by varying its frequency or amplitude.

ADSL   - Asynchronous digital subscriber line. ADSL technology provides very high data transfer rates over standard telephone lines, as much as 70 times faster than a standard modem.

ATB2   - Automated ticket and boarding pass. An ATB2 is different to an ATB in that it has a machine readable, magnetic stripe which holds ticket and boarding information.

bandwidth   - A measure of the amount of data that can be passed through a cable. Bandwidth is one of the constraining factors to the speed of the Internet.

binary   - The digital representation of data. Binary data is encoded using just ones and zeroes, eg. 10011010.

browsing   - Looking at Web sites on the Internet, also called surfing.

call centre   - An operational department within an organization that handles all the telephone enquiries from customers or those seeking information on products and services.

click-through   - The act of using a PC mouse to click a link on a Web page that takes the visitor to another Web site.

CRS   - Computer reservation system. The GDSs used to be called airline CRSs but now the term CRS usually refers to a reservation system internal to an organization.

data-mining   - The technique of analysing the data within sales databases to seek out trends and buying patterns that can form the basis of targeted direct marketing.

digital   - Refers to the encoding of data in a binary format. Data may be any form of electronic information from audio-visual television programming to a simple e-mail or word processing file.

download   - The transfer of electronic data from a third party computer to your own.

DMO   - Destination marketing organization. An organization that is most probably a tourism authority that has, amongst its responsibilities, the task of promoting its destination.

DMS	-	Destination management system. A type of computer system used by a destination marketing organization to facilitate all its business processes such as holding information on local services, providing access to information via kiosks and other information points, facilitating bookings, etc.
domain name	-	An address on the Internet. For example: world-tourism.org is the WTO's domain.
dumb terminal	-	A screen and keyboard connected to a remote computer system. A dumb terminal has no processing or storage capability of its own. It displays information fed to it by a centralised computer system.
e-commerce	-	Electronic commerce. The term used to refer to conducting commercial transactions online.
e-ticket	-	Electronic ticket. An airline ticket that is in all respects the same as a conventional ticket except that there is no physical coupon.
extranet	-	The connection of two or more intranets across the Internet.
gateway page	-	A Web page specifically designed as an entry point into a Web site.
GDS	-	Global distribution system. The term given to the global airline booking systems such as Amadeus, Galileo, Sabre and Worldspan.
home page	-	The page designed as a starting point to further explore a Web site.
HTML	-	Hypertext Markup Language. The script language in which Web pages are written. For example, before a phrase and after the phrase would make it appear in a bold font on a Web page.
hypertext	-	The ability to link from a word or words within a Web page to another page.
IDTV	-	Interactive digital television. Television programming that is transmitted in digital rather than analogue format and that also has a return path so that the viewer can respond to on-screen prompts for information.
intelligent agent	-	Software incorporating decision making algorithms that can act on behalf of its owner.
intranet	-	An internet style system that is only available to users within a single organization.

IP	-	Internet protocol. The computer to computer language used across the Internet.
ISP	-	Internet service provider. A telecommunications company that provides its customers with access to the Internet and other related services.
link	-	Text or image on a Web page that, when the mouse cursor is placed over it and the mouse button is "clicked", takes the user to another Web page.
meta-tag	-	Words serving a special purpose that are part of a Web page but that are not displayed. For example, a 'description' meta-tag will hold descriptive text that will be displayed within many search engines.
modem	-	A device that codes and decodes a digital signal into an analogue signal suitable for transmission over a telephone line.
multimedia	-	Referring to a mix of electronic media such as text, static images and video.
NC	-	Network computer. The modern equivalent of a dumb terminal featuring a full colour screen, keyboard and mouse but otherwise having no processing or storage capability.
net appliance	-	An electronic device that can connect to the Internet.
online	-	Typically used to describe being connected to the Internet but can mean being connected to any remote computer or computer device.
operating system	-	The basic suite of programs used by a computer to allow it to run other software applications. Windows 98, for example, is Microsoft's popular PC operating system.
portal	-	Most often used to describe a Web site used by people as an entry point to the Web. This might be your Internet service provider's home page or a search engine. IDTV services are now trying to also position themselves as portals to the online world.
protocol	-	A common basis of language by which computers can pass data between themselves across computer networks. The protocol of the Internet is IP – Internet protocol.
resolution	-	The degree of detail that can be seen on a computer monitor. Usually measured in pixels - the number of squares on-screen. Most computer monitors have a resolution of at least 800 pixels across the screen by 600 pixels down the screen, ie. 800 x 600.

search engine   -   A Web site that allows the visitor to conduct a search for Web pages containing words that are of relevant interest. For example, Yahoo!, Lycos, Excite, AltaVista.

set-top box   -   An electronic box that connects to a television and provides online access to the Internet or television service.

smart card   -   A credit card sized card that contains a micro-chip to store information such as electronic cash, flight reservation details, identity details.

syntax   -   The layout of wording and punctuation required by a computer to understand what the user is inputting.

systems integration   -   The connection of several computer systems so that they can interact as if they were one system.

unique visitors -   The number of people visiting a Web site regardless of the number of pages they view.

URL   -   Uniform Resource Locator. A URL is the common term used to denote a Web site address.

Web   -   Short name for the World Wide Web, also referred to as WWW. The Web is that part of the Internet that is made up of Web sites.

Web browser   -   A software application used to view Web sites. The two most popular are Microsoft Internet Explorer and Netscape Navigator.

Windows   -   Microsoft's popular operating system for PCs, currently in its Windows 98 version.

XML   -   Extensible Markup Language. An advanced version of HTML that will allow Web sites to pass data back and forth to software applications as if the site was directly connected to the software in use.

APPENDIX 1: ANALYSIS OF 25 'BEST PRACTICE' WEB SITES

The first table below provides a summary of the numbers of sites, out of 25, that included the various features covered by the analysis. The subsequent tables provide a site-by-site tabular analysis of the features of the 25 Best Practice Web sites. By reviewing this information, you should gain an understanding of which are the most common functions of DMO Web sites. This will be an aid to you if you are considering developing a new site or extending an existing one. URLs of all the sites reviewed are contained in the table below.

URLs OF WEB SITES EVALUATED

Evaluated Web Site	Address
Alaska	www.travelalaska.com
Belize	www.travelbelize.org
California	www.gocalif.ca.gov
China	www.cnta.com
Edinburgh (Scotland)	www.edinburgh.org
Egypt	http://touregypt.net
Hawaii	www.gohawaii.com
Ireland	www.ireland.travel.ie
Israel	www.goisrael.com
Malaysia	www.tourism.gov.my
Mexico	www.mexico-travel.com
Morocco	www.tourism-in-morocco.com
Norway	www.tourist.no
Patagonia	www.chileaustral.com
Silkeborg (Denmark)	www.tourist.silkeborg.dk
Snowdonia (Wales)	www.gwynedd.gov.uk/tourism/snowdonia
Tanzania	www.tanzania-web.com
Thailand	www.tat.or.th
Vienna (Austria)	http://wtv.magwien.gv.at

AGGREGATE ANALYSIS OF THE SITES OVERALL

The following table represents an overall analysis of the twenty-five DMO Web sites evaluated. It indicates the frequency with which different site features and functions were recorded. The inclusion of a logo or brand on the home page was the only feature common to all twenty-five of the DMO Web sites indicating the variation in the content of the sites.

Every site contained general information about the destinations they represented but the content and level of detail varied widely from site to site. The features of the sites also varied, but the most common was the inclusion of a list of the main contents on every page of the site, followed by a link to the home page appearing on every page. Both of these features simplify navigation and help prevent users becoming lost within a Web site. Fourteen of the sites included a search to facilitate information retrieval.

More specifically, sixteen of the sites included an interactive database with a search facility to access information about accommodation. Even twelve months ago, such a service would not have been nearly as common. Four of the sites provided the opportunity for users to create virtual brochures, whilst two included an interactive trip planner whereby users could specify their interests and constraints in terms of time and/or money, with a database producing some possible itineraries. Within the next twelve months it is likely that the inclusion of innovative services such as these in DMO Web sites will increase, as part of the trend towards increased sophistication.

Aggregate Analysis of the Functions and Services Offered By 25 DMO Web Sites Evaluated		
Home Page		
- Logo or brand	25	
- Brief textual description of the destination	14	
	Constant	Changing
- Photographic Image of the destination	8	8
- Graphical image of the destination	10	3
- Moving or changing text	8	
- List of internal links	22	
- Have to click on icon or graphic to enter site	4	
- Possibility of selecting the language for the site	13	
- List of awards given to site	4	
- Number of visitors to the site	6	
- E-mail address	9	
- Date last updated	2	
- Local Time	4	
- Possibility of registering or completing an online survey	2	
- Gateways	1	
General Information Contained within the Site		
- Photographs of the destination	19	
- Climate	23	
- Geography	23	
- Topography	23	
- Clothing	12	
- Money	15	
- Shopping hours	20	
- How to get to the destination	22	
- Public transport	21	
- Telecommunications	12	
- Information on sub regions within the destination	23	
- Culture & Customs	22	
	Interactive	Not Interactive
- Suggested itineraries	2	2
- Events	11	9
- Attractions	13	11
- Destination specific activities	13	11
- Maps	12	5

table continued on next page

Features of the Site		
- Web site is available in different languages	14	
- A list of main contents of the site can be seen on every page	21	
- Link back to home on every page	20	
- Site map	8	
- Information on the design of the site	10	
- Statistics on the use of the site	1	
- Virtual, multimedia tours	3	
- Live cams	1	
- List of external links to related sites	19	
- Visitor comments	8	
- Can complete a form to have brochures posted	10	
- Online registration form	2	
Interactive Trip Planner	2	
Can Search database on the basis of . . .		
- How to get to the destination	1	
- What to do at the destination	2	
- Attractions	2	
- Events	2	
- Where to stay	1	
- Transport	1	
- Tours	2	
- Hire	1	
- Where to look for further information	1	
What is included in the list of results generated by the database?		
- Name, address and phone or service provider	2	
- Fax number	2	
- Photographic representation of service provider	2	
- Pricing information	2	
- Brief textual description of service offered	2	
	Direct Link	
	Yes	No
- E-mail of service provider	2	
- URL of service provider	1	1
Virtual Brochures	4	
- Is registering compulsory for first time users?	3	
- Can any information from the site be included ?	2	
- Can the brochure be edited?	3	
Accommodation Information		
● ACCOMMODATION LISTING NOT INTERACTIVE	8	
- One textual list of accommodation options	24	
- Accommodation list divided on the basis of location	5	
- Accommodation list divided on the basis of style Eg hotel	6	
- Accommodation list divided on the basis of price		
● INTERACTIVE DATABASE WITH SEARCH FACILITY	16	
Can search database on the basis of . . .		
- Style of accommodation Ed Hotel, hostel, condominium	14	
- Location within the destination	15	
- Price	6	
- Facilities of accommodation Eg, air conditioning, beach view	4	

154

	Direct Link	
	Yes	No
● INFORMATION PROVIDED ON ACCOMMODATION		
- Address and phone number	23	
- Fax	21	
- Photograph of the accommodation	12	
- Room rates	13	
- Brief textual description of accommodation	13	
- Check in/Check out times	3	
- Child facilities	15	
- Quality accreditation from some governing body	5	
- E-mail	15	1
- URL of accommodation provider	13	
- Online booking through Web site (not supplier Web site)	4	
Search Facility	14	
- Key word search?	13	
- Use directories to search?	3	
On line Shop	5	
- Clothes	2	
- souvenirs	2	
- Books	4	
- maps	4	
- Minimum total order value?	2	
- Do you have to register to shop		
Travel Specials Section	10	

INDIVIDUAL DMO WEB SITE ANALYSIS

The next tables analyse in detail the DMO Web sites reviewed.

FUNCTIONS AND SERVICES OFFERED BY THE WEB SITE					
	Britain	W Australia	Zurich	Singapore	Norway
Home Page					
Logo or brand	√	√	√	√	√
Textual description of the destination	√			√	√
Photograph of the destination	√	√	√	√	
Graphical image of the destination	√				√
Moving or changing text	√	√		√	√
List of internal links	√	√	√	√	
Must click on icon or graphic to enter site					√
Possibility of selecting the language	√		√		
List of awards given to site		√			
Number of visitors to the site		√			
E-mail address	√				
Local Time				√	
Gateways	√				
General Information within the site					
Photographs of the destination	√	√	√	√	√
Climate, Geography, Topography	√	√	√	√	√
Clothing		√	√	√	
Money	√		√	√	
Shopping hours	√		√	√	
How to get to the destination	√	√	√	√	√
Public transport	√	√	√	√	√
Telecommunications	√	√		√	
Information on sub regions	√	√	√	√	√
Culture & Customs	√	√	√	√	√
Suggested itineraries	√	√		√	
Events & Attractions	√	√	√	√	√
Destination specific activities	√	√	√	√	√
Maps	√	√	√	√	√
Features of the site					
Web site available in different languages	√	√	√		√
List of site contents on every page	√	√	√	√	√
Link back to home on every page	√	√	√	√	√
Site map	√	√		√	
Information on the design of the site	√	√		√	
Statistics on the use of the site	√				
Virtual, multimedia tours &/or Live cams				√	
List of external links to related sites	√			√	√
Visitor comments				√	
Can complete form to have brochures sent			√	√	
Online registration form			√		
Interactive Trip Planner		√		√	
Can Search database on the basis of . . .					
How to get to the destination		√			
What to do at the destination		√		√	
Attractions &/or Events		√		√	
Where to stay		√			

FUNCTIONS AND SERVICES OFFERED BY THE WEB SITE

	Britain	W Australia	Zurich	Singapore	Norway
Transport		√			
Tours		√		√	
Hire		√			
Where to look for further information				√	
What is included in the list of results?					
Name, address, phone of service provider		√		√	
Fax number		√		√	
Photograph of service provider		√		√	
Pricing information		√		√	
Textual description of service offered		√		√	
Link to E-mail of service provider		√		√	
Link to URL of service provider				√	
Virtual Brochures	√	√		√	
Registering compulsory for first time users?	√				
Can any info. from the site be included?	√			√	
Can the brochure be edited?		√			
Accommodation Information					
NOT INTERACTIVE					
One list of accommodation options					
Listed on the basis of location					
Listed on the basis of style Eg hotel					
Listed divided on the basis of price					
INTERACTIVE DATABASE & SEARCH	√	√	√	√	√
Can search database on the basis of . . .					
Style of accommodation Ed Hotel, hostel	√	√	√		√
Location within the destination	√	√	√	√	√
Price	√	√	√	√	
Facilities of accommodation Eg, air conditioning	√	√			
INFORMATION PROVIDED ON					
Address and phone number		√	√	√	√
Fax	√	√	√	√	√
Photograph of the accommodation	√	√		√	
Room rates	√	√	√	√	
Textual description of accommodation	√	√	√	√	
Check in/Check out times		√			
Child facilities	√	√		√	
Quality accreditation from governing body	√	√			
Link to E-mail		√	√	√	√
Link to URL of accommodation provider			√	√	√
Online booking through Web site					
Search Facility	√		√		√
Key word search?	√		√		
Use directories to search?	√				√
On line Shop	√		√		√
Clothes	√	√			
souvenirs	√	√			
Books	√	√			√
maps	√	√			√
Minimum total order value?	√	√			
Do you have to register to shop					
Travel Specials Section	√	√		√	

FUNCTIONS AND SERVICES OFFERED BY THE WEB SITE

	Cornwall	Patagonia	Tanzania	Thailand	Ireland
Home Page					
Logo or brand	√	√	√	√	√
Textual description of the destination	√	√	√		
Photograph of the destination	√	√	√		√
Graphical image of the destination	√		√	√	√
Moving or changing text				√	√
List of internal links		√	√	√	√
Must click on icon or graphic to enter site	√				
Possibility of selecting the language				√	
List of awards given to site					√
Number of visitors to the site		√			
E-mail address		√			√
Date last updated		√			
Local Time		√			
Possibility of registering			√		
Gateways					
General Information within the site					
Photographs of the destination	√	√	√	√	√
Climate, Geography, Topography	√	√	√	√	√
Clothing			√	√	
Money				√	√
Shopping hours				√	√
How to get to the destination	√	√	√	√	√
Public transport		√	√	√	√
Telecommunications				√	√
Information on sub regions	√	√	√	√	√
Culture & Customs	√	√	√	√	√
Suggested itineraries				√	
Events & Attractions	√	√	√	√	√
Destination specific activities	√	√	√	√	√
Maps	√		√	√	√
Features of the site					
Web site is available in different languages	√	√	√	√	√
List of site contents on every page	√	√	√	√	√
Link back to home on every page	√			√	
Site map	√		√	√	
Information on the design of the site					
Statistics on the use of the site					√
Virtual, multimedia tours &/or Live cams					
List of external links to related sites		√	√	√	√
Visitor comments	√	√	√		√
Can complete a form to have brochures posted					√
Online registration form					√
Interactive Trip Planner					
Virtual Brochures	√				√
Is registering compulsory for first time users?	√				√
Can any info. from the site be included ?					√
Can the brochure be edited?					√
Accommodation Information					

FUNCTIONS AND SERVICES OFFERED BY THE WEB SITE

	Cornwall	Patagonia	Tanzania	Thailand	Ireland
NOT INTERACTIVE		√	√	√	
One textual list of accommodation options		√		√	
Listed on the basis of location			√		
Listed on the basis of style Eg hotel		√	√		
Listed on the basis of price					
INTERACTIVE DATABASE & SEARCH	√				√
Can search database on the basis of . . .					
Style of accommodation Ed Hotel, hostel	√				√
Location within the destination	√				√
Price					
Facilities of accommodation Eg, air conditioning					
INFORMATION PROVIDED ON					
Address and phone number	√	√	√	√	√
Fax		√	√	√	√
Photograph of the accommodation		√	√		√
Room rates	√				√
Brief textual description of accommodation	√	√	√		√
Check in/Check out times					
Child facilities	√.	√	√		√
Quality accreditation from governing body					
E-mail		√	√		√
Link to URL of accommodation provider		√	√		√
Link to Online booking through Web site					
Search Facility		√	√	√	
Key word search?		√	√	√	
Use directories to search?					
On line Shop	√				
Clothes					
souvenirs					
Books	√				
maps	√				
Minimum total order value?					
Do you have to register to shop					
Travel Specials Section			√		√

FUNCTIONS AND SERVICES OFFERED BY THE WEB SITE					
	Egypt	**Morocco**	**Alaska**	**Mexico**	**China**
Home Page					
Logo or brand	√	√	√	√	√
Textual description of the destination	√			√	
Photograph of the destination					
Graphical image of the destination	√	√	√	√	√
Moving or changing text		√			√
List of internal links	√	√	√	√	
Must click on icon or graphic to enter site				√	√
Possibility of selecting the language		√		√	√
List of awards given to site					
Number of visitors to the site	√				√
E-mail address	√				
Date last updated					
Local Time					
Possibility of registering					
Gateways					
General Information within the site					
Photographs of the destination			√	√	√
Climate, Geography, Topography	√	√	√	√	√
Clothing	√		√	√	
Money	√	√	√	√	√
Shopping hours					√
How to get to the destination	√	√	√	√	√
Public transport	√			√	√
Telecommunications				√	√
Information on sub regions	√	√	√	√	√
Culture & Customs	√	√	√	√	√
Suggested itineraries			√	√	
Events & Attractions	√	√	√	√	√
Destination specific activities	√	√	√		√
Maps	√	√	√		
Features of the site					
Web site is available in different languages		√		√	√
List of site contents on every page		√		√	√
Link back to home on every page	√				√
Site map			√		
Information on the design of the site					
Statistics on the use of the site					
Virtual, multimedia tours &/or Live cams			√		
List of external links to related sites	√	√	√		√
Visitor comments		√	√		
Can complete a form to have brochures posted					
Online registration form				√	
Interactive Trip Planner					
Virtual Brochures					
Accommodation Information					
NOT INTERACTIVE					
One textual list of accommodation options					
Listed on the basis of location					

FUNCTIONS AND SERVICES OFFERED BY THE WEB SITE

	Egypt	Morocco	Alaska	Mexico	China
Listed on the basis of style Eg hotel					
Listed on the basis of price					
INTERACTIVE DATABASE & SEARCH			√		
Can search database on the basis of . . .					
Style of accommodation Ed Hotel, hostel		√	√		√
Location within the destination		√	√		√
Price					
Facilities of accommodation Eg, air conditioning					
INFORMATION PROVIDED ON					
Address and phone number	√	√	√	√	√
Fax		√	√	√	√
Photograph of the accommodation		√			√
Room rates					√
Brief textual description of accommodation		√	√		
Check in/Check out times					
Child facilities		√		√	√
Quality accreditation from governing body					√
Link to E-mail		√			
Link to URL of accommodation provider					
Online booking through Web site					
Search Facility	√			√	√
Key word search?	√			√	√
Use directories to search?					√
On line Shop			√		
Clothes					
souvenirs					
Books			√		
maps					
Minimum total order value?					
Do you have to register to shop					
Travel Specials Section	√	√			√

FUNCTIONS AND SERVICES OFFERED BY THE WEB SITE					
	Norway	Israel	Snowdonia	Belize	Edinburgh
Home Page					
Logo or brand	√	√	√	√	√
Textual description of the destination	√	√	√	√	
Photograph of the destination		√	√	√	√
Graphical image of the destination	√	√		√	
Moving or changing text	√				
List of internal links		√		√	√
Must click on icon or graphic to enter site	√		√		
Possibility of selecting the language			√		
List of awards given to site				√	
Number of visitors to the site					
E-mail address			√	√	√
Date last updated					√
Local Time				√	
Possibility of registering					
Gateways					
General Information within the site	·				
Photographs of the destination	√	√	√	√	√
Climate, Geography, Topography	√	√	√	√	√
Clothing		√		√	
Money		√		√	
Shopping hours				√	
How to get to the destination	√	√	√	√	√
Public transport	√	√	√	√	
Telecommunications				√	√
Information on sub regions	√	√	√	√	√
Culture & Customs	√	√	√	√	
Suggested itineraries					
Events & Attractions	√	√	√		√
Destination specific activities	√	√	√	√	√
Maps	√	√	√		
Features of the site					
Web site is available in different languages	√		√		
List of site contents on every page	√	√		√	√
Link back to home on every page	√	√	√	√	√
Site map					
Information on the design of the site				√	√
Statistics on the use of the site					
Virtual, multimedia tours &/or Live cams				√	
List of external links to related sites	√	√	√		√
Visitor comments					√
Can complete a form to have brochures posted		√	√		√
Online registration form		√			
Interactive Trip Planner					
Virtual Brochures					
Accommodation Information					
NOT INTERACTIVE		√			
One textual list of accommodation options		√			
Listed on the basis of location					

FUNCTIONS AND SERVICES OFFERED BY THE WEB SITE

	Norway	Israel	Snowdonia	Belize	Edinburgh
Listed on the basis of style Eg hotel					
Listed on the basis of price					
INTERACTIVE DATABASE & SEARCH	√		√	√	√
Can search database on the basis of . . .					
Style of accommodation Ed Hotel, hostel	√		√	√	√
Location within the destination	√		√		√
Price				√	√
Facilities of accommodation Eg, air conditioning			√	√	
INFORMATION PROVIDED ON					
Address and phone number	√	√	√		√
Fax	√	√	√	√	√
Photograph of the accommodation			√	√	√
Room rates			√		√
Brief textual description of accommodation			√	√	
Check in/Check out times					
Child facilities			√	√	
Quality accreditation from governing body			√		√
Link to E-mail	√	√	√	√	√
Link to URL of accommodation provider	√	√	√	√	
Online booking through Web site					
Search Facility	√			√	
Key word search?				√	
Use directories to search?	√				
On line Shop	√				
Clothes					
souvenirs					
Books	√				
maps	√				
Minimum total order value?					
Do you have to register to shop					
Travel Specials Section					√

FUNCTIONS AND SERVICES OFFERED BY THE WEB SITE					
	Hawaii	**Vienna**	**Silkeburg**	**California**	**Malaysia**
Home Page					
Logo or brand	√	√	√	√	√
Textual description of the destination		√	√	√	√
Photograph of the destination		√	√	√	√
Graphical image of the destination	√	√	√	√	
Moving or changing text			√		√
List of internal links	√	√	√	√	
Must click on icon or graphic to enter site				√	
Possibility of selecting the language	√	√	√	√	√
List of awards given to site					
Number of visitors to the site		√		√	
E-mail address		√			
Date last updated					
Local Time	√				
Possibility of registering					√
Gateways					
General Information within the site					
Photographs of the destination	√		√		√
Climate, Geography, Topography	√		√	√	√
Clothing		√		√	√
Money	√		√	√	
Shopping hours	√	√		√	
How to get to the destination	√	√		√	
Public transport	√	√		√	
Telecommunications	√			√	
Information on sub regions	√		√	√	
Culture & Customs	√	√		√	
Suggested itineraries		√			
Events & Attractions	√	√	√	√	√
Destination specific activities	√	√	√	√	√
Maps		√		√	
Features of the site					
Web site is available in different languages	√	√	√		√
List of site contents on every page	√	√	√		√
Link back to home on every page	√	√	√		√
Site map			√	√	√
Information on the design of the site		√	√	√	
Statistics on the use of the site					
Virtual, multimedia tours &/or Live cams				√	
List of external links to related sites	√	√	√	√	√
Visitor comments		√	√		√
Can complete a form to have brochures posted	√		√	√	
Online registration form					√
Interactive Trip Planner					
Virtual Brochures					
Accommodation Information					
NOT INTERACTIVE				√	
One textual list of accommodation options					
Listed on the basis of location				√	

FUNCTIONS AND SERVICES OFFERED BY THE WEB SITE

	Hawaii	Vienna	Silkeburg	California	Malaysia
Listed on the basis of style Eg hotel					
Listed on the basis of price					
INTERACTIVE DATABASE & SEARCH	√	√	√		√
Can search database on the basis of . . .					
Style of accommodation Ed Hotel, hostel	√	√	√		
Location within the destination	√	√	√		√
Price					√
Facilities of accommodation Eg, air conditioning					
INFORMATION PROVIDED ON					
Address and phone number	√	√	√	√	√
Fax	√	√	√	√	√
Photograph of the accommodation	√			√	√
Room rates	√	√			√
Brief textual description of accommodation	√			√	
Check in/Check out times	√				
Child facilities	√	√		√	√
Quality accreditation from governing body					
Link to E-mail	√	√		√	√
Link to URL of accommodation provider	√	√	√	√	
Online booking through Web site					
Search Facility	√	√		√	
Key word search?	√	√		√	
Use directories to search?					
On line Shop					
Clothes					
souvenirs					
Books					
maps					
Minimum total order value?					
Do you have to register to shop					
Travel Specials Section					

APPENDIX 2: INDICATIVE COSTS TO PARTICIPATE ONLINE

DMO INTERNET WEB SITES

It is perfectly possible to develop an attractive Web site for a tourism board or any other destination marketing organization for under $10,000. This will not be a database driven site but may be very adequate if all the DMO is trying to achieve is to place a limited amount of static information about its destination on the Web. The revenue cost of such a site would be the cost of hosting by an Internet service provider. This would be in the region of $1,000 per annum.

However, most DMOs Web sites carry far more information than is practicable to host on a static site. The pages for these sites are created dynamically, information being pulled into the pages from a database as visitors require it. This type of site requires a server permanently connected to the Internet. The server will hold the database of information and will build the pages as they are needed for display. The cost of such a system depends on the size of database and number of site visitors.

A basic database driven system might cost as little as $3,000 for the server and $2,000 per annum for the connection to the Internet plus, of course, the cost of designing the site, from about $10,000. A major destination with millions of visitors to a Web site containing many thousands of pages might expect to develop a technology infrastructure costing $500,000 with direct (non-staff) running costs of $250,000 per annum. This would be the type of cost incurred for a site offering fully interactive capabilities. Much more can be spent if a DMO wishes to offer functions such as interactive mapping technology and personalise electronic brochures. The most comprehensive Web sites will require an investment of millions of dollars.

DESTINATION MANAGEMENT SYSTEMS

It is difficult to provide definitive guidance on the costs of a DMS. It is clear from the case studies in Chapter 5 that there is no such thing as a 'standard' DMS. Different DMOs have had quite different requirements, according to their objectives, resources, scale and range of activities, organizational structure, etc. Costs will also vary substantially between destinations. Thus in planning a new DMS, data relating to existing DMSs must be carefully interpreted in terms of potential relevance.

Costs must be divided into various broad headings, relating to:

- The technical infrastructure of computers and network communications
- The database management system and related software
- The digital database content
- Standard 'off-the-shelf' software
- Specialist software for DMO functions – eg. accommodation reservations

- Project management
- DMO staff training and development
- Awareness and skills training for tourism suppliers.

Under some of these headings, particularly the first, there will be substantial capital costs. There will also be ongoing (operating) costs under all of the headings. The following examples provide a broad indication of costs that might be incurred for new database driven DMSs in different circumstances, in Western Europe, excluding costs of staff (except project management) and premises.

Scenario	Capital Costs US$'000	Operating Costs US$'000 per annum
DMS for a local destination with 2,000 bedrooms and one information office, using off-the-shelf software with a limited range of functions, including information office activities and a simple Web site, but excluding kiosks and call centre.	250-350	125-75
For a region with (say) 20,000 bedrooms, development of a DMS with a wide range of marketing, sales, visitor services (including reservations) and office functionality.	4,000-8,000	2,000-3,000
For an NTO with 10 offices abroad, developing a Web-based system with limited original software for internal communication, for electronic marketing to consumers and for industry and intermediary communication, working with selective databases and with no reservation function (except click-through from a Web site)	750-1,250	400-600

Such broad estimates leave a lot of questions unanswered. For example, PCs and other hardware are required by DMOs for many purposes, but are clearly essential to the operation of a DMS. Should their purchase and maintenance be attributed to the DMS budget in part or in total?

There are more complex issues of ownership and structure that also affect cost allocation and the net costs to DMOs. The case studies demonstrate a considerable variation in DMS structures, ranging from the largely privately-owned Gulliver to the DMO-owned, but commercially self-standing, TIScover at the comprehensive DMS end; and through the NTO-funded and controlled operations in Canada and Finland to EU-supported programmes in Namibia and the South Pacific. A common feature of all of these has been the requirement for substantial public funds but there is a clear trend towards the involvement and use of private capital in DMS implementation under the growing belief that public/private partnerships in this field may provide excellent returns in the short to medium term.